THE
PROPHET
OF LOVE

Meditations on the Book of Hosea

Chris Liff

WESTBOW
PRESS®
A DIVISION OF THOMAS NELSON
& ZONDERVAN

WestBow Press books may be ordered through booksellers or by contacting:

WestBow Press
A Division of Thomas Nelson & Zondervan
1663 Liberty Drive
Bloomington, IN 47403
www.westbowpress.com
844-714-3454

ISBN: 978-1-6642-7058-9 (sc)
ISBN: 978-1-6642-7059-6 (hc)
ISBN: 978-1-6642-7057-2 (e)

Library of Congress Control Number: 2022911823

Print information available on the last page.

WestBow Press rev. date: 07/27/2022

Introduction

There can be no subject in the whole world more vitally important or exhilarating than the love of God for sinful humanity. The wonder of God's love is forever proclaimed to us in the life, death, and resurrection of Jesus Christ. But the writers of the Old Testament undoubtedly also delighted in the knowledge of God's love. Their collective message was the promise of unimaginably great love and hope revealed to a world filled with injustice and despair. They proclaimed God's powerful love promised in the coming of Christ, who would deliver the world from its desperate condition.

The book of the prophet Hosea is unique in its portrayal of God's love. Hosea candidly presents his own frustrating love life as a means of demonstrating God's perfect love. His preaching declared God's astonishing patience, faithfulness, and mercy to sinful people. Hosea is the prophet of love!

The purpose of this present study of Hosea's writing is to assist contemporary Christians in understanding and benefiting from Hosea's rich insights into God's dealings with His people. Hosea's book is a spiritual treasure for all Christians today. It exhorts and encourages us to faithfulness and perseverance in our daily walk with Christ.

Hosea is in some ways a difficult book to read. It is set in an ancient culture that is very different from our own. It is filled with long descriptions of the sins of Hosea's nation and people. It warns of the dreadful chastisement of God soon to come as a result. These passages remind us of our own spiritual struggles in living for God in a fallen world.

We need the message of Hosea! In the depths of our sin and despair, Hosea shows us how God dramatically proclaims His mercy. He calls us to repentance and restores us to fellowship with Him. We are reminded that serving God with clean hands grows out of a purified heart. Hosea proclaims the transforming power of God's love! He teaches us that God is eternally faithful to fulfill His glorious promises of peace and security. These are promises that can only become reality by faith in the finished work of Jesus Christ on our behalf. Hosea's book points us to Christ and thus displays the main theme of the whole Bible. Hosea's message is the power of God's love to bring spiritual life and rich blessings to the whole world.

This study consists of thirty-eight meditations on the teaching of Hosea. These should be read slowly, thoughtfully, and prayerfully. It is probably best to read one meditation per day. They were written with the intention of personal study. However, it may be useful to discuss these thoughts with others. They have profitably been used in a small group study at the author's church.

It is imperative to read the passage from Hosea at the beginning of each meditation. Keep your Bible open to that portion of Hosea as you read. Consult the verses referenced in the meditation. The meditations are only there to help you understand the meaning of Hosea's words. Ask God to speak to your heart through His word. It is God's Spirit who gives understanding and applies the word in our lives.

There are many difficult passages in Hosea, and some where the experts are not in agreement about their meaning. On those passages I have set forth what prayerfully seems to me to be the best interpretation, but without justification or discussion of other views.

My main sources of study are commentaries by Keil, Calvin, James Boice, David Allan Hubbard, Matthew Henry, and Charles Feinberg. Also helpful was Michael P. V. Barrett's *Love Divine and Unfailing: The Gospel According to Hosea* (Phillipsburg, NJ: P&R, 2008), and Anthony Selvaggio's *The Prophets Speak of Him* (Webster, NY: Evangelical Press, 2006).

I owe a vast debt of gratitude to the kind folks at Covenant Presbyterian Church in Barre, Vermont, for their patience and encouragement in this project.

My sincere prayer is that those who read these pages will find the same rich comfort in the love of God that I have found in writing them.

A Scandalous Marriage
Hosea 1:2–3

PROPHET MARRIES PROSTITUTE! It was the gossip column sensation of the year, circa 760 BC. What could Hosea have been thinking? Was this God's wonderful plan for his life? Wouldn't this bring disgrace to his family and alienate his friends? What would the neighbors say? He even claimed he was a prophet and that God told him to do this! Was he insane? How could he expect to serve as God's faithful spokesman after exhibiting such poor judgment?

Yet God's command was clear: "Go, take to yourself a wife of whoredom" (Hos 1:2). Why would the Lord give such a scandalous order to His prophet, undoubtedly bringing into his life great shame, ridicule, and anguish? He makes the lesson perfectly clear: "For the land commits great whoredom by forsaking the Lord" (Hos 1:2). God would use the unfaithfulness of Hosea's wife to vividly portray the unfaithful rebellion of Israel to their God. And through Hosea's persistent love for his wayward wife, God would show forth the wonder of His infinite, unfailing love in redeeming to Himself sinful men and women.

The Lord had spoken through Moses to the people of Israel six hundred years before Hosea. At the summit meeting at Mt. Sinai, the Lord had extended the covenant He had previously made with Abraham, Isaac, and Jacob to the nation descended from them. God established a covenant relationship with Israel, declaring that those whom He had delivered out of bondage in Egypt were now called to be His very own possession, set apart for rich blessing by His presence among them. In return, He alone would be their God, claiming the worship and loyalty of their hearts.

Though not directly stated by Moses, God was picturing His covenant with Israel as a marriage relationship. He declares His love in choosing His people (Dt 7:7–8) and He desires first of all their love in return (Dt 6:5). He reveals Himself as the God who is faithful to His promises (Dt 7:9), and requires in return a commitment of faithfulness from Israel (Dt 11:13). He is the jealous God (Dt 4:24) who will not share the heart of His people with another. He is like a husband to His people, faithfully providing for (Dt 7:12–15) and protecting (Dt 7:17–24) them. Moses gave a solemn warning that any worship or reliance on other gods is the equivalent of spiritual prostitution (Ex 34:15–16; Dt 31:16), bringing severe judgment on such unfaithfulness to their covenant God.

Hosea's marriage is a parallel of God's marriage to Israel. The pain and anguish that Gomer's eventual unfaithfulness brings to Hosea are reminders of God's intense desire for the undivided love of His covenant people. For Israel had failed to continue in the covenant love of their God. They had offered their hearts in worship to the false gods of the surrounding peoples, abandoning of the love of God who had claimed them as His very own treasured possession. Hosea bluntly calls this spiritual whoredom. Much of what follows in Hosea's writing is a detailed indictment of the marital unfaithfulness of the nation. Yet, under God's direction, Hosea's attempt to restore his relationship with Gomer also reveals God's infinite grace and mercy in reconciling wayward sinners to Himself.

Hosea's scandalous marriage points powerfully to Jesus Christ in His love for His church. Christ also chooses for Himself a bride who is unlovely, guilty, and defiled. He gives all He has for her, loving her all the way to death to gain her love. He cleanses her to make for Himself a glorious bride, pure and spotless (Eph 5:25–27).

While Hosea's heroic love seeks to capture the affection of His wife, Christ's infinitely powerful love purifies our souls and overflows in our lives. Hosea's love points us to the far greater love of Christ, the only hope for a fallen hopeless human race.

Hosea is the prophet of love. He shows forth by his words, but also by his life, the faithful unfailing love of God that restores and heals broken lives and relationships.

Grace through Humility
Hosea 1:2–3

"GO, TAKE TO yourself a wife of whoredom" (Hos 1:2). How could God give such a humiliating command to a godly young man whom He called to be His prophet? Would God desire that our sons or our church leaders seek such a marriage? Wouldn't such a shameful relationship disqualify a man for service in God's kingdom?

God, in His wondrous and wise working in the world, chose at times to direct His prophets to act in humiliating, even disgraceful ways. A vivid example is in Isaiah 20, where God commanded His prophet to walk in public for three years with his buttocks exposed as a portrayal of God's coming judgment against Egypt. Through Hosea's marriage, God was visibly demonstrating the guilt of spiritual prostitution of the whole land in forsaking the Lord (Hos 1:2). As Gomer's sin brought shame to her husband, so Israel's sin brought shame to their God. How hard-hearted and rebellious these people must have been! God in His wisdom found it necessary to bring before them a shocking example in order to show the depth of their depravity.

But was God calling his prophet to commit a sinful act? Gomer had been intimate with other men, but not in the manner of permanent, cherishing, and sacrificial commitment that marriage entails. From a human point of view Hosea's marriage may have been extremely unwise and undesirable, but it was not adulterous.

Yet it was gracious! Hosea was calling his wife to leave her sinful lifestyle and to enter into the committed love and care of her husband. He takes to himself someone depraved and undesirable, brings her into his family, and seeks with her a relationship of mutual kindness, intimacy, and blessing. He offers her mercy and compassion when she is deserving of only scorn and shame.

Is this not a reminder of God's gracious, merciful calling to Israel throughout her history as God's chosen people? God declared through Moses that His blessings to the people of Israel were not because of their righteousness, for they were a stubborn, rebellious people (Dt 9:6–7). Yet the Lord set His heart in love upon them and chose them as His people (Dt 10:15). His call to Abraham was to leave behind an idolatrous, pagan culture and to live under the covenant care of the one true God. He called the tribes of Israel out of bondage in Egypt to be His treasured possession, separated from the world and consecrated to serve Him alone.

What a glorious picture Hosea gives us of God's grace and kindness through our Lord Jesus Christ to His people in every generation! God calls us out of unbelief, out of the darkness of sinful rebellion and hatred, into the light of His love and faithfulness made known to us in Christ. We are all like Gomer. None of us are lovely in His sight, none are desirable or righteous or pure, but Christ has set His eternal love upon a vast multitude. These He also has redeemed and called into His kingdom of righteousness (Col 1:13–14), to be the praise of His glorious grace (Eph 1:6).

Hosea's humility in his marriage reminds us that the grace of Christ comes to us through His humiliation. He who is the eternal God, robed in majesty, ruling in power, worthy of all praise, honor, and glory, humbled Himself and became obedient even to death on a cross. Christ was despised and rejected by men, dying in utter shame and humility, but was raised up from death in great glory. So He is able to deliver us out of the humiliation of our sin, and bring eternal blessings of spiritual life to all who trust in Him.

Terrible Tidings

Hosea 1:4–5

THE BIRTH OF children is a cause of great joy and celebration, but the children born to Hosea and Gomer brought terrible tidings to the nation Israel. Hosea was instructed by the Lord to give his children prophetic names. Not only Hosea's marriage but the names of his children spoke clearly of the dreadful spiritual state of Israel in his day.

God gave Hosea's firstborn the name Jezreel, a name that conveyed three dire predictions concerning the future of the people of the nation Israel. The descendants of their king would be punished, their kingdom would come to an end (Hos 1:4), and their military strength would be defeated (Hos 1:5). Jezreel means "God scatters." God would destroy the kingdom and scatter the people in exile over the nations of the earth. This clearly was not a joyous or a popular message!

Yet God gave clear warning of this severe judgment through the prophets He sent to the people of Israel. All the Old Testament prophets whom God inspired to write lived in the period from 800

BC to 400 BC. The dominant historic events in those centuries were destruction and exile, first of the northern kingdom of Israel by the Assyrians (722 BC), and then of the southern kingdom of Judah by Babylon (587 BC). Through the message of these prophets, God left no doubt as to His reason and purpose for these tragic events. Hosea 1:2 speaks of their great whoredom in forsaking the Lord. They had brought the worship of the false gods of the surrounding nations into their religious life. Hosea likened this to the violation of a marriage covenant by adultery.

After Moses led the people out of Egypt, God entered into a covenant relationship with Israel, establishing them as His people and promising to be their God (Dt 29:12–15). The covenant demanded from His people heartfelt loyalty and faithfulness in worshiping only the one true God. He also declared that if they abandoned the covenant and worshiped other gods, they would be overthrown and uprooted from the land (Dt 29:24–28). God's prophets following Moses consistently reminded Israel of God's covenant claim on His people and they gave strong warnings of the consequence of covenant unfaithfulness.

Hosea began his prophetic ministry during the reign of Israel's King Jeroboam II (793–753 BC). Jeroboam's long reign (see 2 Kings 14:23–29) was characterized by military strength, by which he was able to deliver Israel from its enemies and extend its borders. This powerful king brought peace, security, and prosperity to the land. However, he also continued in the idolatrous worship that had plagued Israel for two hundred years. The apparent strength of the nation was undermined by spiritual, social, and moral decay, as the words of the prophets Hosea and Amos so clearly describe. The nation belonging to the Lord, but now relying on other gods for survival, could not long endure.

God indeed brought terrible judgment upon the nation that He Himself established as His very own people. This stands as a vital lesson to all those who claim to believe in the God of the Bible. God's people, called by His covenant mercy, are able to stand in His presence only by faith and must continue to serve Him in covenant faithfulness. We rely on His mercy and power to persevere in exalting the true God alone with all our being. In dependence on His strength we strive to be diligent in honoring Him in our worship, in prayer, and in seeking to live according to His commands. God in His mercy knows the unfaithfulness in our sinful hearts, in constantly wandering away from our Creator and Redeemer, pursuing other lords, trusting in gods of our own making. Hosea's warning is needful for all those who profess to follow the one true God. Covenant unfaithfulness will lead to spiritual destruction. Our spiritual life, begun by the goodness and power of God, must continue to grow and mature in sincere devotion and reliance on His life-transforming grace.

But our amazing God does not allow the story to end with the terrible tidings of judgment! Many centuries after Hosea, God brought to Israel another child whose coming completely fulfilled to His people all the eternal blessings of God's covenant promises. On the night on which that child was born, a mighty angel appeared in heavenly glory, proclaiming, "Behold, I bring you good tidings of great joy, which shall be to all people. For unto you is born this day in the city of David, a Savior, which is Christ the Lord" (Lk 2:10–11 KJV). God sends the joyful good news that in infinite grace He has sent a Savior who bore our sinful rebellion on the cross. Only by the grace of Christ are we purified from our sin and given new hearts, eager to do what is right in His sight. He writes His law on our hearts and minds and is sanctified as Lord in our hearts. Covenant faithfulness is accomplished for us in Christ's finished work; it is applied to us by His Spirit, so that we may walk in righteousness before Him all our days. God's final word of glorious glad tidings to the

The Blood of Jezreel

Hosea 1:4–5

GOD GAVE THE name Jezreel to Hosea's firstborn son. He explains the reason in Hosea 1:4: "I will punish the house of Jehu for the blood of Jezreel." Who was this Jehu?

Hosea's prophecy began (Hos 1:1) during the reign of King Jeroboam II (793–753 BC). Jeroboam's Great-Grandfather Jehu led a rebellion, killed two kings, shed the blood of any who were loyal to them, and seized the throne for himself. Beginning at the royal palace at Jezreel, he slaughtered the family and descendants of Ahab and Jezebel, the wicked rulers of Israel, in 841 BC (2 Kings 9:30, 10:11). The dynasty of Jehu began with appalling bloodshed.

Hosea, at the beginning of his prophetic ministry (ca. 760 BC), boldly declared that God's punishment because of the bloodshed at Jezreel was soon to come upon the descendants of Jehu. This was a prophecy that the reign of King Jeroboam would soon come to an end! The Valley of Jezreel (Hos 1:5) is a strategic plain between the mountains of Judah and those of Galilee. It is a convenient passage for invaders from the East. It has been the site of many significant battles. As Jehu's reign began at Jezreel, so Hosea predicts that his dynasty will end in defeat in this same valley. Hosea's words to the nation are bold and dire.

This presents some confusion, because according to 2 Kings, Jehu's rebellion was both commanded (2 Kings 9:7) and commended (2 Kings 10:30) by the Lord. Jehu was God's instrument to bring judgment on the wicked reign of Ahab. Why was Jehu's house now punished for deeds that God had ordered and approved?

Perhaps the answer is explained in 2 Kings 10:31: "But Jehu was not careful to walk in the law of the Lord, the God of Israel, with all his heart. He did not turn from the sins of Jeroboam, which he made Israel to sin." (The reference is to Jeroboam I, the first king of Israel [930–909 BC], who had rebelled against the kingdom of David and Solomon and instituted idolatrous worship in the northern kingdom.) Jehu's house continued in the same sins for which God punished the house of Ahab. God's appointed king was supposed to lead the people in devotion and faithfulness to the Lord. Jehu found it much easier to lead a bloody massacre than to lead the people in peace and righteousness. Ultimately, his actions were motivated by desire for his own glory and power. He was serving his own agenda and not that of the God who had placed him in a position of leadership. God judges not only our actions but also our motives. Do we accomplish the work He has given us in this world for our own gain, or to advance God's kingdom and glory? Doing the right thing with the wrong motive is never pleasing in the sight of God.

Jeroboam II was a powerful king and his reign was a long period of military strength, peace, and prosperity. Yet he continued to do evil (2 Kings 14:24) and lead Israel into false worship. It is astonishing how quickly Hosea's prophecies of doom and destruction coming upon the kingdom of Israel were fulfilled, as briefly recorded in 2 Kings 15–17. Jeroboam was succeeded by his son Zechariah, who after only six months was murdered by Shallum, ending the reign of the house of Jehu. Over the next thirty years there were five more kings, four of whom were deposed and killed. During that time there were at least four invasions by the Assyrians, the world's superpower. The kings of Assyria conquered the area around the Valley of Jezreel in 733 BC (2 Kings 15:29) and again in 724 BC (2 Kings 17:5; Hos 10:14). The kingdom of Israel came to its end with the fall of Samaria (722 BC) and exile of the people. It seems likely that Hosea was still alive to witness this dreadful fulfillment of his prophecy.

One thing of which Hosea is firmly convinced is that the God of Israel is the sovereign Lord over kings, nations, and history. God is well able to bring down to destruction kingdoms and rulers that exalt their own power and commit crimes of violence against their people while ignoring the rule of the God of heaven. Hosea's amazing courage and conviction in delivering a message of severe judgment against his own people and nation displays a steadfast trust and reliance on the faithfulness and power of his God.

Indeed, God promises to sweep away and bring to nothing all who reject the reality of His rule and lordship over their existence. Yet this same God is preparing a heavenly country (Heb 11:16) for all those who by His grace seek to honor Him and submit to His righteous rule in this world. Other prophets spoke of an eternal kingdom established by the God of heaven (Dan 2:44) that would crush all the kingdoms of the earth and of a king who would come to Israel (Zec 9:9) who would rule to the ends of the earth. The voice of the angel left no doubt who that king would be (Lk 1:31–33). Jesus, the Son of the most high God, would reign over His covenant people forever. The consummation of His kingdom

Strange Names

Hosea 1:6–9

MANY PARENTS IN the modern world seem to search for unusual names for their children, but surely none would dare to give the strange names that Hosea, at the Lord's command, gave to his last two children. His daughter was named Lo-ruhamah (meaning "No Mercy") and his son Lo-ammi ("Not My People"). Can we imagine children growing up bearing such names?

God gave these names to Hosea's children as a prophecy of the spiritual ruin of His own children of Israel. Hosea's firstborn was given the name Jezreel, a prophecy of the coming destruction of the king and kingdom of Israel. Such severe judgment would have been shocking and unthinkable to the people of Israel, who were confident of their status as the chosen people of God. So now the names of the next two children send a clear explanation: Israel's people have broken the covenant, and lost their gracious standing as the people of God. They have been unfaithful to their covenant-keeping God. God speaks of their spiritual whoredom and forsaking the Lord (Hos 1:2). By rejecting the God of the covenant they forfeited the blessings of the covenant.

God, through Moses, had declared His covenant love to Israel. He had shown the people great mercy by delivering them out of bondage in Egypt. The essence of the covenant relationship is that He would be their God and would take them to be His people. He promised this while they were still in Egypt (Ex 6:4–8) and proclaimed it again at Mount Sinai (Ex 19:4–6). He declared Himself to be "a God merciful and gracious, slow to anger, and abounding in steadfast love and faithfulness" (Ex 34:6). Through the blessings of walking according to all His laws (Lev 26:3–12) He would confirm His covenant with them. He would dwell among them, walk with them, and be their God. He also renewed the promise of covenant blessing (Dt 29:12–15) to Israel as they were on the verge of entering the promised land. How glorious and precious are these blessings of the abiding grace and kindness of the living God who reigns over all the universe!

And how appalling to turn away from the God who promises such rich blessings, to serve the demands of the culture around us and the sinful desires of our heart. We so easily set created things up as our gods and order our lives according to the dictates and priorities of the world around us, a world with no regard for the glory and honor of our Creator God.

God gave these strange names to Hosea's children to proclaim that Israel had broken the covenant relationship by turning to other gods. As He was no longer their God, so they were now "Not My People." As they refused to repent of their rebellion, so His chastisement would come with "No Mercy." As Israel was living in the manner of the pagan nations surrounding them and serving their pagan gods, so He would treat them as pagans. Israel would no longer be a people set apart unto God from the world. In exile He was sending them among the nations, returning them to the pagan world. Nor would he forgive them, for they refused to repent of their waywardness, rejecting His mercy.

By contrast, God does promise to show mercy to the southern kingdom of Judah (Hos 1: 7). He gave them righteous kings such as Uzziah and Hezekiah (Hos 1:1), who honored the God of Israel and walked in His ways. He saved Judah not by military might but by His direct intervention. Samaria was conquered by the Assyrians (722 BC), but Jerusalem was miraculously delivered from their power (701 BC) by God's mighty hand (2 Kings 19:35).

Yet how rich and wonderful is the grace of our God, who ultimately did fulfill His gracious purpose for the people of Israel by preserving and restoring them as a nation. He spoke a glorious promise through another prophet, Isaiah, who lived at the same time as Hosea. Isaiah promised a miraculous birth of another son, whose name would be called Immanuel, which means "God with us" (Is 7:14). He further spoke of this son, saying that His name would be called "Wonderful Counselor, Mighty God, Everlasting Father, Prince of Peace" (Is 9:6). God's promise was not to abandon this world in all its sin but to draw near in wondrous mercy, to be God with us.

When hundreds of years later this child was born, the angel directed that His name should be Jesus (which means "Jehovah saves") because He would save His people from their sins (Mt 1:21). Of Jesus it is declared that "there is no other name under heaven by which we must be saved" (Acts 4:12). Because He has accomplished everything necessary for our salvation, He has been highly exalted and given the name above every name; at the name of Jesus every knee should bow and every tongue confess that Jesus Christ is Lord (Phil 2:9–11). By believing in Him we have life in His name (John 20:31). What a wondrous work God has done. He has taken away our names of rejection and judgment and replaced them with the name of Jesus, the name of salvation, of God with us!

Jesus is the promised Son whose name is wonderful. God sent Him as the mediator of a new and more excellent covenant (Heb 8:6) and to guarantee (Heb 7:22) to His people all His covenant blessings. In the New Testament letter to the Hebrews we learn of the essence of this new covenant (Heb 8:8–12), that He will be our God and we will be His people. He will be merciful toward our iniquities and remember our sins no more. What wondrous love, that the blessings of the covenant that Hosea declared to be lost to the people of Israel are restored to us in Christ. Now He promises to write His laws on our hearts and minds so that we may all know the Lord and abide in His love, faithfully serving Him in this world. For it is God's grace that calls us into covenant relationship; that grace also keeps us faithful to His covenant. His covenant love teaches us to rely on Him for salvation and to persevere in our love and service to Him.

In Christ we receive a new name (Rev 2:17) and a new identity (2 Cor 5:17). We are baptized into the name of Jesus Christ for the forgiveness of our sins (Acts 2:38). In baptism, His name is placed upon us as a sign that we belong to Him. Our entire existence and all our endeavors are dedicated under the name of Christ Jesus (Col 3:17). That name is our glory, and in it we bring glory to God in this world (1 Pet 4:16).

Christians live under not a strange name but a glorious, wonderful name—God with us! For in Christ we are a people He has claimed as His very own. He has called us by His name and bestowed on us rich mercy. Let us then forever treasure His covenant blessings to us. And let us be diligent to always walk in His ways and delight in His kindness, giving to Him all honor and thanks, for His mighty power is able to keep us in His grace throughout this life and forever.

Restored by Mercy
Hosea 1:10–2:1

IF WE ENJOY stories with sudden, unexpected twists in plot, we should be delighted with the glorious, good news God declares through Hosea in these verses. The first word of Hosea 1:10, "Yet," signals an earthshaking change from judgment and destruction to restoration and blessing.

This transition from judgment to blessing is so shockingly abrupt that we must wonder if God is contradicting Himself. It appears that He makes one promise and then in the next breath promises the exact opposite! In Hosea 1:9 He says, "You are not my people," but in Hosea 1:10 He calls them "children of the living God." In Hosea 1:7 He says, "I will have no mercy to forgive them," but in Hosea 2:1 He says, "You have received mercy." God is true in all He says and does, but we struggle to understand how these statements can both be true.

This apparent contradiction in the promises of God is actually the central theme in the whole book of Hosea! At least seven times in Hosea's prophecy, after speaking at length about the coming judgment for Israel's sin, he gives a very sudden and unexpected promise of great blessing and hope. This is intended to shock us into considering the amazing grace of our God in His dealings with sinful humanity. He is the righteous judge who must punish sin, yet His purpose is not condemnation. All of scripture declares God's desire to gather a vast multitude of people to Himself, redeeming and purifying them to love and serve Him with joyful, thankful hearts. Hosea's audacious theme is powerfully confirmed in the words of Jesus in John 3:17: "For God did not send his Son into the world to condemn the world, but in order that the world might be saved through him."

Many of the Old Testament prophets were given the unpleasant task of announcing destruction and exile for the nations of Israel and Judah. But these same prophets were also given a message of future restoration, blessing, and peace! Israel's sin was very serious, rejecting God's covenant relationship and blessings. As promised by Moses, such disobedience would surely result in severe chastisement from the hand of the Lord. However, this judgment was not to be total or final. As promised in Dt 30:1–10, this severe chastisement was to lead to repentance and forgiveness. Although the people had broken the covenant, God remained faithful to His promise to bring glory and blessing to the whole world through His mercy shown to Israel. Humanity's unfaithfulness could not destroy the saving purpose of God. God's mercy prevails over the sin of His people!

Hosea's words point beyond the coming judgment to a glorious future restoration by the mercy of God. Hosea's children were given names containing dire prophecies of coming destruction upon the nation. But now Hosea speaks of the children of Israel restored to rich blessing by God's mercy. Those who God had declared were no longer His people (Hos 1:10) will be called children of the living God! This shocking reversal is not only predicting the return of Israel to their promised land but also a spiritual restoration of worship and devotion to the Lord. Although they had been unfaithful to their God, He now promises to adopt them again as His children. They will be born of the Spirit, born from above. The God they had forsaken will restore them in astonishing mercy. The remnant of the nation He had severely chastised will become the seeds of His family of adopted children whom He will call to Himself from every nation on earth.

God really did bring about the miraculous deliverance of the people of Israel from captivity and restored them to their promised land. But Hosea speaks here of a far greater deliverance, the rich spiritual blessings to God's people that can come only by the mercy of our Lord Jesus Christ. The promise that those who are not His people will become His children includes the Gentiles! The blessings of redemption are promised to all—both Jews and Gentiles—who trust in Christ as Savior and Lord, calling upon Him alone for salvation. Israel's people, decimated by invasion and exile, will become so great they cannot be numbered! God will restore to Himself a new Israel, a vast multitude from the whole of humanity, to live under His covenant blessings.

And these children will be gathered together under one king (Hos 1:11). The ten tribes had rebelled against the house of King David, and formed the separate nation of Israel. But now all the people of God would be reunited in obedience to the king God had appointed. King Jesus, in great power and mercy, will unite Jews and Gentiles in one family. It is only through faith in Christ, the eternal King of Israel, that this great restoration of Israel can come to pass. Christ, who rules the nations of the world with a rod of iron, will gather together the Gentiles into the household of God.

And great shall be the day of Jezreel (Hos 1:11). Those who had been scattered into exile by defeat in the Valley of Jezreel were now to be returned from exile as one people. Jezreel means "scattered" but also in the sense of scattering seeds to plant a crop. The people of Israel would be an abundant harvest. They would come up from the land as a nation raised up to new life out of judgment and slaughter. God will have a plentiful harvest from all nations and peoples. Hosea proclaims that this will be a great day, a day for rejoicing and celebration!

The celebration continues in Hosea 2:1, where all God's faithful children rejoice in this great deliverance of His people and confess their faith to one another. God has reversed the curse! "Not my people" becomes "my people"; "no mercy" becomes "have received mercy" (Hos 2:1). The children of the curse become children of the blessing, united in God's new family. God graciously brings to a remnant of Israel a spiritual restoration. In rich mercy He fulfills His covenant promises to a vast people whom He calls from every nation. Let us rejoice greatly!

How vast beyond our comprehension is the conquering mercy of God! God's promises do not fail. He remains faithful despite our unfaithfulness. He continued His purpose to bring into the world a Savior through the people of Israel. He fulfilled His covenant promise in our Lord Jesus Christ, by whom He defeated the power of sin over the human race. He has redeemed to Himself a vast multitude, purifying them from sin and making them a people to be His treasured possession, eager to do His will. As God's mercy preserved and restored Israel, so His mercy will bring safely into His eternal kingdom all who look to Christ to deliver them from this present evil age. Christians are a new humanity, restored to spiritual wholeness and peace by God's mercy in Christ.

Children of the Living God

Hosea 1:10–2:1

WE MUST MARVEL at how very bold Hosea is as he declares God's covenant love for Israel. God once again would adopt a remnant of the people of Israel as His children from their exile in pagan lands. They will be not only a people chosen for His very own and not only a nation called by His name. They will now be members of His family, beloved children of the living God. Restored from exile, they will find that the blessings they have gained are far greater than those they lost. How great are the riches of God's kindness and love in restoring sinners to Himself!

The New Testament apostles are also audaciously bold. They used the words of Hosea in speaking of God's adoption of the Gentiles by faith in Christ! When the apostles wanted to show how the Old Testament scriptures taught that God's eternal purpose was to bring salvation to people from every nation, they turned to this passage in Hosea. Paul quotes Hosea in Romans 9:25–26 to declare the will of God to call to Himself in Christ people not only from the Jews but also from the Gentiles. These who believe in Christ for salvation he calls vessels of mercy, prepared beforehand for glory, to whom He would make known the riches of His glory (Rom 9:23–24). The Gentiles who previously were not God's people will now be called children of the living God. Peter, speaking to predominantly Gentile Christians in 1 Peter 2:10, also makes reference to Hosea. He states that those who were not a people are now the people of God. They who once had not received mercy now have received mercy through the gospel of Christ. What Hosea said concerning Israel, the apostles declared to be true of Gentile as well as Jewish believers in Christ.

Christ's apostles revealed the big picture of God's working out His purposes in human history. God chose Israel as the stage upon which He would show mercy to the whole world. He announced His purpose from the very beginning, in His call to Abraham, saying "In you all the families of the earth shall be blessed" (Gen 12:3). In Psalm 2:8 the Lord says to His Son, "Ask of Me, and I will make the nations your heritage, and the ends of the earth your possession." Psalm 67:1–3 says that God's blessings are given to Israel so "that your (God's) ways may be known on earth, your saving power among all nations." This is done in order that all the peoples on earth will give praise to the God of Israel. The Lord speaks to His servant (Is 49:6) saying, "I will make you as a light for the nations, that my salvation may reach to the end of the earth." In Daniel's great vison of Christ, "one like a son of man" (Dan 7:13–14) is presented before the Ancient of Days. "And to him was given great dominion and glory and a kingdom, that all peoples, nations and languages should serve him." The summary of the Old Testament is God's promise to send a deliverer to Israel, who is Christ, the Savior of the whole world.

The apostles clearly saw Hosea's promise of God's restoration of Israel as fulfilled in His grace of salvation to the whole world through Jesus Christ. Israel's return from the captivity was a mighty miracle of God's sovereign power over the nations. As God had once delivered His people out of slavery in Egypt under Moses, He now brought about a new exodus out of bondage and exile. God showed great mercy to Israel in gathering them out of the nations of exile and establishing them again as His people. But this was only a partial fulfillment of Hosea's words. The world needed a greater deliverance, a fuller exodus, which only came through Christ.

Hosea speaks of "one head" (Hos 1:11) appointed over them, their king, who would gather His people together and lead them once again to the promised land. Christ is the head of a new humanity, His church, and promises to safely lead all who trust in Him into a far more glorious kingdom. Jesus told His disciples, "It is your Father's good pleasure to give you the kingdom" (Lk 12:32). Paul writes to a mixed Gentile and Jewish church in Colossians 1:13–14: "He has delivered us from the domain of darkness and transferred us to the kingdom of his beloved Son, in whom we have redemption, the forgiveness of sins." "Christ always leads us in triumphal procession" (2 Cor 2:14). In Christ "we overwhelmingly conquer through Him who loved us" (Rom 8:37 NASB). Christ is our Passover lamb sacrificed for us (1 Cor 5:7), our strong deliverer by whom God has set us free from bondage to sin and death. God has given us the great victory of resurrection hope through our Lord Jesus Christ (1 Cor 15:57). Hebrews 11:13–16 speaks of our journey by faith to "a better country ... a heavenly one" (Heb 11:16), "looking forward to the city that has foundations, whose designer and builder is God" (Heb 11:10). The apostles of Christ understood that Hosea's prediction of spiritual restoration could only be accomplished by the redemption provided by the death of Christ.

God's purpose was to bring that redemption to the Gentiles as well as to the Jews! God punished Israel's idolatry by sending them among idol worshipers. But then He chose to show forth His infinite compassion and mercy to idol worshipers. He condemned their idolatry and drew the hearts of Israel back to the living and true God. Thus He demonstrated His will to bring a vast multitude of idol worshipers from every nation and people under His blessings of covenant grace in Christ.

And this work of God's amazing grace continues to this day! In Romans 11:30–32, Paul summarizes God's purpose in the world for this present age: that the Gentiles who were once disobedient to God have now received mercy, so that through that mercy the Jews in their disobedience might also receive God's mercy.

"For God has consigned all to disobedience, that He may have mercy on all. Oh, the depth of the riches and wisdom and knowledge of God!" (Rom 11:32–33).

Hosea's Marital Disaster
Hosea 2:2–5

THE JOY AND triumph to which Hosea's family life pointed at the end of chapter 1 is suddenly shattered by the worst possible real-life nightmare in chapter 2. Hosea's love for his wife has been crushed and his delight in her brought down to intense grief. Gomer has abandoned her marriage to Hosea and returned to her former life of prostitution. She has gone after other lovers (Hos 2:5) for pleasure and profit. Hosea's marriage lies in ruins (Hos 2:2) and they are no longer united as husband and wife. He and his children plead with Gomer (Hos 2:2) to turn away from her blatant immorality. He warns (Hos 2:3) that her course of life will surely result in disgrace, futility, and deprivation. Her actions will bring upon her children (Hos 2:4–5) nothing but shame and trouble. What should have been a relationship of faithful union and mutual delight has become shattered wreckage.

This disaster in the prophet's personal life is given as a picture of the greater disaster in Israel's spiritual life. The message is really about Israel's great whoredom (Hos 1:2) in forsaking the Lord.

This becomes clear later in chapter 2, where Israel's devotion and religious feasts (Hos 2:8, 13) to Baal are condemned. As Gomer abandoned her husband and went after her lovers (Hos 2:5), so also Israel went after her lovers (Hos 2:13) and forgot the Lord. Hosea's anguish at his wife's behavior is a vivid portrayal of God's outrage at the rejection of His love so lavishly bestowed on His covenant people of Israel.

We can well imagine the medley of strong emotions that afflicted Hosea, knowing that his love had been rejected and cast aside as something worthless. Hosea is deeply grieved by his wife's unfaithfulness. He is indignant that one who is very precious has been stolen from him. He undoubtedly is humiliated and is justifiably angry. Despite intense hurt, his love for Gomer continues. He pleads with her (Hos 2:2) and remains hopeful that she will return to him (Hos 2:7).

God's love had similarly been spurned by His chosen people Israel, and their worship given to another. God uses Hosea's anguish to give us a clear picture of His deep desire for the heartfelt love of His people. He wants us to understand what an enormous injustice occurs when the adoration of our hearts that He so richly deserves is given to another. God uses human marriage to illustrate the intimate commitment and union declared to His people in His covenant promises. God is a personal God, and the scriptures frequently express His intense longing and zeal for His bride, the church. He is profoundly grieved and indignant over the unfaithfulness and waywardness of His covenant people.

God has loved His church with an everlasting love. He has demonstrated His love for all time in sending His Son to die for the sins of His people. No greater love can be found anywhere in the universe. His love is unmerited, costly, sacrificial, and self-giving, an eternal and unchangeable commitment to bring us extraordinary blessing. Yet in our sin we so often set our desire on other lovers, follow other voices, and pursue the gods of this world. Tragically, we reject His love and are unfaithful to the one who called us to be His own treasured possessions.

May all God's people be ever mindful that His love is our greatest treasure. May we steadfastly walk in His love and delight in His gracious presence. So may our every moment be dedicated to returning to Him from our poor hearts that wondrous love with which He has loved us in Christ Jesus.

Love That Will Not Let Go

Hosea 2:5–13

HOSEA UNDOUBTEDLY FELT helpless and frustrated at his wife's unfaithfulness. Not so with God! He reveals His strategy to restore His wayward wife, Israel. We see the loving heart of our God for His bride as He actively pursues His straying people. His faithfulness endures forever! His is a love that will not let go

Yet, tragically, the people of Israel had let go of their love for God. Five times in these verses Hosea speaks of Israel's pursuit of "her lovers." God's covenant love had been freely bestowed upon Israel's people, but they were now giving their heart's affection to other gods. Israel provoked God's jealousy by taking the religious celebrations of God's goodness and dedicating them to Baal (Hos 2:8, 13, 16, 17). The nations surrounding Israel believed they were dependent on their pagan fertility cult worship to bring forth their livelihood from the land. Israel, seeking to ensure its abundant harvests, had adopted a form of Baal worship along with its worship of Jehovah. Israel was calling on a pagan god to supply the material blessings that could come only from the hand of God. Israel's great sin was taking the glory rightfully belonging to God and giving it to a false god, which is no god at all.

God reveals His strategy for restoring the hearts of His people to Himself. Most impressive in these verses are the numerous "I will" statements. God's hand is powerfully working in the lives of His people with increasing severity, to call them back to Himself. In order to restrain them He will build a wall of thorns (Hos 2:6), take back His blessings (Hos 2:9), and uncover their shame with no one to rescue them (Hos 2:10). He will put an end to their feasting (Hos 2:11), lay waste their harvest (Hos 2:12), and punish their idolatrous worship (Hos 2:13). God will not share His glory with another. His love binds His people to Himself and he will not let go. He will use whatever means necessary to create in us pure hearts consecrated to Him alone.

The first step of God's strategy is to show how sinful rebellion always leads to frustration and futility (Hos 2:6–7). He will build walls to block our path and frustrate our plans. We will lose our way and the desires we pursued will not reach fulfillment. His aim is to bring us to realize that all our rich blessings come only from the loving care of our God.

God's second step is to remove material blessings (Hos 2:8–9). When the good gifts of God that fill our lives are used to worship the false gods of our culture and in pursuit of our sinful desires, He will take them back. We will not find satisfaction in all we have; we will endlessly be seeking more and never have enough. How hard it is for us to learn that our greatest happiness comes only from the hand of God, from whom all blessings flow.

Third, He will expose our sinful desires and actions (Hos 2:10), and they will bring us shame before the watching world. If we profess to be God's chosen people but fail to honor Him in thought, word, and deed, our hypocrisy will bring about disdain and ridicule among unbelievers. Our unfaithfulness to the God of grace and mercy will be regarded as lewdness by those false "lovers" whom we have embraced. God is determined to turn our wayward hearts to joyful obedience that responds to His abundant love.

The final step in God's strategy of restoration (Hos 2:11–13) is to remove all joy and comfort from our worship of the false deities of our own desires and imaginations. When we substitute the love of created things for the worship of the Creator, our misplaced devotion will not bring us fulfillment. Our religious observance will become dull and tiresome. God's rich blessings, which should inspire heartfelt worship, will become like a dense and pathless forest when credited to other lovers (Hos 2:12), leading only to danger and frustration. God severely punished and brought to an end Israel's false worship in the invasion and exile by the Assyrians.

How precious is the liberating love that God has ordained to pour out into our sinful hearts (Rom 5:5). He powerfully calls us into His family and transforms our lowly lives into glorious trophies of His grace. His power will also guard our hearts and preserve us for life in His eternal kingdom. The covenant relationship God has graciously initiated with His people demands our faithfulness and loyalty to God, our sovereign Lord. He alone is to receive our worship, and our lives are to be consecrated to His service. We acknowledge that His gracious blessings in our lives are completely unmerited, and that we are dependent upon His mercy for every good thing. We are committed to living after the manner of His will as revealed in His word, because we know the amazing power of His love for us in Christ Jesus.

If we forget His gracious love, God will relentlessly pursue us to restore to Himself the love of our wayward hearts. If we set our hearts to worship and serve the desires and priorities of the surrounding culture that are opposed to God's revealed will, He will persistently remind us of the claim of His love on our existence. He will remove or bring to futility those false gods that are claiming our affection. He will have our hearts all for Himself. His love will never let us go.

The Winner of Hearts
Hosea 2:14–17

WHAT WILL GOD do about His wife (Israel) who has gone after other lovers and forgotten Him (Hos 2:13)? The beautiful answer in Hos 2:14 will shock and surprise us. He will court her with tenderness and win her love again! He will speak kindly to her, proclaim His love for her, and shower her with gladness and hope. He will draw her heart to Himself until she again exclaims, "my husband" (Hos 2:16). How amazing is the grace of our God whose love endures forever, whose faithfulness continues to all generations.

God here is proclaiming a new exodus, where He calls Israel once again out of bondage to be His very own possession. Bringing the people into the wilderness (Hos 2:14) is not sending them into exile. It is leading them out of their captivity. God once led His people by Moses through the great and terrifying wilderness (Dt 8:15) in order to humble and test them (Dt 8:2), so they could see how the Lord carried them safely all the way to the promised land (Dt 1:31). So now God will again preserve and restore a remnant of His people out of exile. He will remain faithful to His promises for Israel despite their sinful disobedience. God triumphs over the hearts of His people in delivering them from the power of sin. The exile was not a punishment to destroy the people of Israel but a chastisement to lead them to repentance, to purify and restore them in single-hearted devotion. God uses trials and affliction to draw the hearts of His people closer to Himself, that they should seek His grace and live for His will and honor. The Lord disciplines those He loves and chastises every child He receives (Heb 12:6).

Yet how gentle, with what extraordinary kindness, is His gracious work of reclaiming for Himself the love of our hearts. He says, "I will allure her ... and speak tenderly to her" (Hos 2:14). He is like a lover who, having lost the affection of His beloved through no fault of His own, now seeks once again to convince her of the enduring commitment of His love. How wondrous that our God, the sovereign Lord who ordains the affairs of men and angels, comes in mercy to win the hearts of His people.

God will turn the trouble arising from Israel's sin into a door leading to the hope (Hos 2:15) of all His goodness and strength. *Achor* means "trouble," and in that valley Achan was punished for bringing trouble on Israel by his disobedience (Joshua 7:25). The curse of Achan's sin was removed from the nation in order to restore the rich glory of God's presence among them. So will God now redeem Israel from their sinful rebellion and open the way to a future of glorious blessing.

God will indeed perform this great miracle of restored hearts. Those who had forgotten their gracious God will now "answer as in the days of her youth" (Hos 2:15). How easy it is for us to forget the love we had at first (Rev 2:4). How we need this gracious promise to restore our hearts to respond to His love! At Mt. Sinai, in the youth of the nation of Israel, the people had pledged "All that the Lord has spoken we will do, and we will be obedient" (Ex 24:7). This clearly was the right answer, but their hearts were woefully lacking in ability to carry out what they promised. Now it is God who promises to grow in their hearts the loyalty and commitment that can only come through the transforming power of His grace. Our entire life must rely fully on the grace of God to move our hearts to persevere in love and desire to serve Him acceptably.

And our restored hearts will worship the living and true God. We worship that which our heart affections are set upon. Our mind will be centered on (Hos 2:17) what our heart worships, and our mouth will delight to speak of what our heart treasures. When He wins our hearts for His very own, He will remove from our mouth and mind even the memory of the false gods to which we gave our wandering allegiance. God is capturing the hearts and reclaiming the worship of His people (Hos 2:16).

In addressing their God as "my Baal" (Hos 2:16), Israel was degrading the true and living God to nothing more than the one who filled their stomachs. Their worship of Baal consisted in a constant reminder of their dependence on rain to produce their crops. Baal was not a god who ruled over storms; he was the storm. Instead of calling on the Lord who rules over nature, they made nature their lord. God declares that Israel will no longer call Him "my master" but rather "my husband." He intensely desires the love of His bride and transforms her relationship to Him from abject slavery into heartfelt union and loyalty.

How is it possible for our sinful, rebellious hearts to be transformed into sanctuaries of His praise and glory? Paul says in Romans 5:5 that we may rejoice in the hope of glory because "God's love has been poured into our hearts." We know this love because "while we were still sinners, Christ died for us" (Rom 5:8), and being "justified by His blood ... we shall be saved by him from the wrath of God" (Rom 5:9). So we who were God's enemies have been "reconciled to God by the death of His Son" (Rom 5:10). Thus we now "rejoice in God through our Lord Jesus Christ" (Rom 5:11). God's amazing love in Christ is still seeking and winning the hearts of men and women throughout the whole world for Himself.

And I Will Make for Them a Covenant

Hosea 2: 18–23

IN ESTABLISHING HIS covenant, God presents glorious hope for sinners! When God establishes a covenant in scripture it is as if God were saying, "I will make you a deal so good you can't possibly refuse it." Of course in human interaction, if the deal seems too good to be true, it probably is. But God's covenant deals are both true and exceedingly wonderful. He faithfully promises us grace to embrace His truth and persevere in His love all the way to heavenly glory.

God's promise in Hosea 2:18 is to restore to the people of Israel His covenant blessings, which were lost because of their unfaithfulness in forsaking the Lord. In Hosea 2:14–17, God declares that He will not forsake His unfaithful bride but will renew His kindness to her and win her love again. His will is to draw repentant sinners into a bond of mutual union, loyalty, and faithfulness. Then, in Hosea 2:18–23, as God's covenant of steadfast love transforms our hearts to desire above all else

His presence and approval, we will find our lives filled with unimaginably glorious blessings.

First and foremost, Hosea speaks of a covenant of restored union and communion with the living God. "You shall all know the Lord" (Hos 2:20). He will have mercy on "No Mercy" (Hos 2:23). "Not My People" shall become His people, and they shall say "You are my God" (Hos 2:23). He reveals a restored relationship in which he now pours forth all the heavenly blessings of fellowship with the living God. God's covenant of redemption comes in powerful grace to bring sinners into a relationship of trusting obedience and love with the Creator and Lord of the universe.

This is a covenant established in God's sovereign will and free grace. The numerous "I will" statements in these verses proclaim that all God's covenant promises come by His initiative and powerful decree. He does not say, "I will make a covenant with them," but "I will make a covenant for them" (Hos 2:18). His covenant declares that His favor rests upon those whom He has adopted as His very own people and brings to them the highest blessing and benefit. His promises encompass our every desire and fulfill our every need with the grace of reconciliation and communion with the God who created us.

This is a covenant of peace (Hos 2:18)! God promises to abolish all that is dangerous to us, whether from nature or from men. But this must flow out of the destruction of our spiritual enemies, which are the source of all evil and strife in the world. The covenant with the beasts and birds represents the restoration of the created order destroyed by the curse of the ground (Gen 3:17) due to man's sin. Isaiah 11:6–9 speaks of this: "The wolf shall dwell with the lamb ... The nursing child shall play over the hole of the cobra ... They shall not hurt or destroy in all my holy mountain, for the earth shall be full of the knowledge of the

Lord as the waters cover the sea." True peace can only come from the removal of the effects of sin. Abolishing war has proved to be far beyond the reach of humanity, but God's "I will" speaks of the hope of a world where God's powerful grace conquers and transforms human hearts. "Nation shall not lift up sword against nation, neither shall they learn war anymore" (Is 2:4) will only come as the nations are drawn by grace to worship the Lord and learn His ways. The promise to lie down in security (Hos 2:18) can never be fully certain in a sinful world. Surely these promises all point to the hope made sure to us only in Christ: a new heaven and new earth, where righteousness dwells (2 Pet 3:13).

For this is a covenant of eternal blessings. He says, "I will betroth you to me forever" (Hos 2:19). Three times He uses the phrase "in that day" (Hos 2:16, 18, 21), speaking of a future time when God's great covenant grace will be fully revealed. All these glorious riches will be established in history but will continue throughout future ages to grow more abundant and precious. Surely the final fulfillment of "in that day" is in the holy city, the new Jerusalem (Rev 21:1–3), where God Himself will dwell among men and be their God.

This is a marriage covenant. The promise to "betroth you to me" (Hos 2:19) carries all the commitment of affection, care, and permanence of a man taking to himself a bride. This is a perfect marriage! It is a union characterized by righteousness, justice, steadfast love, mercy, and faithfulness. All those things that the people of Israel were not, in their previous disobedience, God will be to them, and he will work into their hearts and lives in relationship with Him. In marriage, two are united as one. That is a profound mystery, but it refers to Christ and the church (Eph 5:31–32). The immensity of God's love, in entering into a union of eternal commitment and delight with sinful people, is wondrous beyond all comprehension. And it is a marriage that will last forever! God's faithfulness endures forever; His grace in Christ to His people will last for eternity. The final fulfillment must surely be at the marriage supper of the lamb (Rev 19:7–9), where the bride is clothed in the righteousness of Christ and is welcomed into rich blessing with great joy under the eternal reign of the great King.

And it is a covenant of abundant blessing. The people of Israel, formerly scattered in exile and now sown as seeds to grow in the land (Hos 2:23), learns that it is God, not Baal, who provides for all their needs. As they desire their crops to grow, the crops request nutrients from the land, the land requests rain from the heavens, and the heavens request the hand of God to open all these blessings. God surely will answer the prayers of His people and from heaven send forth every provision for our needs. Jezreel can mean "God sows," and the heavens and earth and the crops will answer Jezreel, because it is the hand of God that sends forth blessing. God's promised answer of abundant provision for all our needs goes far beyond physical needs in the present world to every spiritual blessing in the heavenly places in Christ (Eph 1:3). The final harvest of God's blessing for us is from the tree of life (Rev 22:2), which bears its fruit each month, and whose leaves are for the healing of the nations.

Hosea certainly is speaking here of the miraculous restoration of Israel after the coming exile. God will turn His people away from the treason of idolatry by His redeeming power, capturing their hearts for Himself and restoring them to the blessings of their land of promise. However, these promises also speak of a restoration far beyond the return from the exile. For He proclaims everlasting spiritual blessings. These promises can only point forward to a far greater deliverance from our bondage to sin through our Lord Jesus Christ. These are blessings of the new covenant, fulfilled in Christ the mediator of the new covenant. Paul was a minister of the new covenant (2 Cor 3:6) to the Gentiles, a ministry of God's reconciliation of the world to Himself in Christ, not counting their sins against them (2 Cor 5:19). In reconciling rebellious Israel, God shows His mercy not only to Israel but to the whole world! His will is to bring about spiritual birth for a vast multitude from every nation, who will rejoice to confess Him as their God.

How vast, how overwhelming is the boatload of blessings God promises to His redeemed people! God's covenant restoration of lost sinners is a reality for all who are in Christ, who came that we "may have life and have it abundantly" (Jn 10:10). Let us rejoice with Paul: "And my God will supply every need of yours according to his riches in glory in Christ Jesus" (Phil 4:19).

Love as the Lord Loves Israel

Hosea 3:1–3

HOSEA'S TRAGIC MARRIAGE reaches a new low point. Gomer has departed from him and is pursuing an adulterous lifestyle. Her adultery has led her into slavery to another man who is exploiting her body for monetary gain. This is a hideous selfish "love" that possesses for profit. His "love" for her is such that he is willing to sell her for the price of a slave. How appalling are the consequences of falling into a sinful, rebellious lifestyle!

Now Hosea, at God's command, must pay a price to buy Gomer out of slavery. He is to renew his love for her, not only in paying the ransom price but in the far more costly heartfelt forgiveness and reconciliation. Hosea may well have protested that it would be humanly impossible to love in the face of such rejection and humiliation as he had endured in his broken marriage. And his protest would be right! God's words to him speak of a supernatural kind of love that far exceeds the ability of the human heart.

Hosea is to again show his love to his wife even as the Lord loves the children of Israel (Hos 3:1). God's forgiving, pursuing, restoring love for Israel has just been marvelously described in Hosea 2:14-23. Now Hosea's love is to depict God's love in real life. Once again, Hosea's relationship with Gomer is prophetic, this time through restoration. Hosea's marriage is a living demonstration of God's infinite wondrous love for unfaithful Israel. God shows us His love for sinful men and women, love far beyond human ability or comprehension.

What an amazing picture we are given here of the powerful love of God for sinners. This is, first of all, a love that is unmerited. We in our sin are like Gomer in God's sight: unlovely, disgraced, and rebellious. We, like Israel, have set our hearts to love other gods, the gods of our own pride and sensual worldly pleasures. The objects of our heart's devotion are often as trivial as raisin cakes! (Jeremiah 7:18 and 44:19 speak of cakes that were offered in worship to the queen of heaven. The raisin cakes in Hosea 3:1 appear to refer to Israel's delight in their ceremonies of idolatrous worship.) How little do we deserve God's kindness, yet His love is an active power that takes initiative to seek us in our lostness. This is love that forgives, love that shows compassion for the unlovely, love that restores broken relationships. It is a costly love, a love that gives from the heart and provides healing and blessing for all the deepest needs of the soul. It is a love of eternal commitment and intimacy. It is heavenly, divine love. Where else but in God's love can we ever find such glorious blessing?

Hosea's obedience extends well beyond merely buying back his wife. He renews his marriage vows with her (Hos 3:3). Though she is technically his slave, his love liberates her from her past sordid lifestyle into the security of committed intimacy. She shall dwell with him many days under his care and protection. The duration is open-ended, a permanent unending union. The affection of her heart is to be his, exclusive of all others, and he pledges the same commitment to her. This amazing, unanticipated restoration mirrors God's promised redemption of His people from slavery to sin (Hos 2:23). But His grace abounds still further, also bringing them under all the blessings of security and fellowship in the family of the true and living God.

For Hosea's love here demonstrates divine love, the far greater love by which God has redeemed for Himself a vast multitude from every nation and people on the earth (Rev 5:9). The price Hosea paid to win his wife's love again was relatively trivial compared with the infinitely great price Jesus paid for the ransom of His people, the price of His blood poured out and His life given over to death. Peter speaks of this ransom of God's people in 1 Peter 1:18–19: "Knowing that you were ransomed from the futile ways inherited from your forefathers, not with perishable things such as silver or gold, but with the precious blood of Christ, like that of a lamb without blemish or spot." And He has made us into "a chosen race, a royal priesthood, a holy nation, a people for his own possession" (1 Pet 2:9). Hosea's loving redemption of his wife points us to a far greater redemption in Christ's love for His people. His is the truly amazing love that powerfully forgives, restores, and establishes us securely in the household of God for all eternity.

Seeking David, the King

Hosea 3:4–5

THE GLORY OF Hosea's prophecy is that he not only talks about God's love, he also shows us God's love. In chapters 1–3, Hosea's love for his wayward wife vividly portrays God's glorious, merciful love for His rebellious covenant people. In Hosea 3:4–5, the restoration of Hosea's marriage is an exact parallel of God's promised restoration of Israel. Israel's immense unfaithfulness will incur tragic loss, but God's infinite mercy will bestow a far more glorious and blessed renewal.

In these concluding verses of chapter 3, the themes of the whole book are presented. In Hosea 3:4, a severe chastisement upon the nation for "many days" is prophesied, serving to remove all that is displeasing to God. In Hosea 3:5, by God's grace this cleansing will bring about repentance and a spiritual restoration leading to future glorious blessings. Their wicked, ineffectual kings shall be removed, and in their place the true children of Israel will bow before the promised king of glory who will reign in true righteousness. In a miraculous transformation, the hearts of those who had forsaken their God will return and seek the Lord their God and the righteous reign of the Messiah promised through David, their king.

Hosea 3:4 describes the coming destruction and exile of Israel's kingdom. The people's king, their worship, and their priests will all be shattered. By their rejection of the rule of the one true God, all the strength and security He had given them was rendered useless. They will be left without king or prince. They will be subject to a foreign power with no ruler, leader, or defender to help them. God will also put an end to their idolatrous worship. Their sacrifices had long been offered to idols (1 Kings 12:28–32). The pillars were memorials raised to false gods (Ex 23:24; Lv 26:1). The *ephod* was worn by the priests as a symbol of authority and was used to obtain divine guidance (1 Sam 30:7–8). But the ephod also became associated with the private worship of household gods (Judges 17:5) and was used in seeking prosperity and fruitfulness from those gods. God swept away in the exile all these emblems of sinful rebellion. Their idols were utterly worthless in delivering them from their enemies. God will bring judgment upon all that are falsely called gods and robs Him of His glory.

Hosea 3:5 proclaims the promise of a spiritual restoration. The children of Israel are those who in true faith return to Him and repent of their rebellion. In worship they will seek the Lord, calling upon His sovereign majesty for their deliverance. In reliance on His mercy, they shall seek future glorious blessings promised through David, their king. They will come in fear to the Lord and to His goodness. So they will not only seek the Lord but they will find Him and receive from Him infinite mercy and healing power.

When the remnant of Israel's people returned from exile, they did reject idolatry and worshiped the Lord only. However, the words "in the latter days" (Hos 3:5) point far beyond the return from exile to the complete fulfillment of God's purpose of a restored humanity in the coming of Christ.

How can Hosea combine seeking the Lord with seeking King David? David had died more than two hundred years before Hosea wrote, so this must refer to a continued reign of David's descendants. God had spoken the promise in 2 Samuel 7:12–16 that a descendant of David would reign on his throne forever. God would be a father to him and would call him His son. This promise is quoted (Heb 1:5) and applied to Christ, the divine Son, who made purification for our sins and is seated forever in heavenly majesty. Peter's sermon (Acts 2:30-31) assures us that David's descendent, the risen Christ, is reigning not only on David's throne but at the right hand of God. We can only seek the Lord by seeking David's greater son, Christ!

The ten tribes of the northern kingdom of Israel had rejected the rule of the kings descended from David and thus separated themselves from the promise of the Messiah. But now God extends His promise of grace and forgiveness, not only to a remnant of the tribes of Israel but to all, Jews and Gentiles together, who will come and bow before the majesty and dominion of Christ. The mercy He showed to faithless Israel is a prophecy of the riches of His kindness in Christ to the idol worshipers throughout the whole world. The "children of Israel" (Hos 3:5) are all who are of the same faith as Abraham, those who are heirs of the promise given to Abraham that he would be the father of many nations (Rom 4:16–17).

Hosea speaks here of a spiritual restoration that is desperately needed by all of humanity. In our sin we have offended the holy God who created us and we are separated from His blessing and favor. Our highest priority in life must be to seek reconciliation with the God who created us and to live in the light of His glory and grace. A new spiritual life is promised to all who seek the Lord. This can only be found in the gift of salvation through Christ's death for our sins and His resurrection triumph over sin and death. At His gracious invitation, we may come to the Lord and seek His favor. We must seek the living God only by seeking Christ, who is the greater King promised to David.

Hosea says we must come in fear to the Lord and to His goodness. This is not a fear of Him because of His wrath. Those who fear His wrath do not seek Him; they seek to hide from Him, to push Him out of their lives. But we may come to Him only because Christ has delivered us from the wrath of God. In His goodness we are not driven away from Him but drawn near to seek Him in reverence and awe. We seek the Lord in hope because we know that He is only good, and always good, and in Christ He is good to us and good for us. We come in fear to the goodness of the Lord. We understand that His goodness to us is as great as His majesty and power. We come in reverence of His divine majesty and in awe of His mighty power. But we come in amazement that He has willed to show us all the blessings of His goodness and kindness in Christ.

A Marriage in Ruins

Hosea 4:1–3

CHAPTER 4 OF Hosea begins in a court of law. The court is in session. The judge takes His seat and delivers a charge against the people of Israel. The judge is also the plaintiff, and He brings a charge against His adulterous wife. The judge is suing for divorce!

Hosea 4:1 contains the threefold accusation: "There is no faithfulness or steadfast love, and no knowledge of God in the land." Clearly no marriage could endure for long under such conditions. The covenant people, chosen and called to be God's very own treasured possession, have turned to other lovers. They have failed to return the love so richly shown them in God's covenant promises. They have abandoned any heart commitment to intimate communion with the Lord, any delighting in His kindness or honoring His majesty. Surely Hosea gives us the picture of a beautiful relationship gone horribly wrong. God's gracious relationship with His covenant people has become a marriage in ruins.

But Hosea doesn't stop there. Hosea 4:2 says that loss of love for God has brought about lack of love for humanity. It results in all manner of horrible crimes in defiance of God's moral laws. Hosea 4:3 speaks of dreadful consequences in the land as environmental and economic devastation becomes the dominant rule of life.

But can we really envision the God who ordains and sanctifies marriage as pursuing a divorce? God Himself speaks through latter prophets of the tragic rebellion of His people in terms of divorce. In Jeremiah 3:8 the prophet speaks of Judah's sinful treachery using the example of Israel's downfall, saying, "She saw that for all the adulteries of that faithless one, Israel, I had sent her away with a decree of divorce." Also Isaiah 50:1: "Thus says the Lord: 'Where is your mother's certificate of divorce with which I sent her away? ... For your transgressions your mother was sent away.'" And James 4:4, 5 gives a severe warning against spiritual adultery: "You adulterous people! Do you not know that friendship with the world is enmity with God? Therefore whoever wishes to be a friend of the world makes himself an enemy of God. Or do you suppose it is to no purpose that the Scripture says, 'He yearns jealously over the spirit that he has made to dwell in us'?" God as a husband intensely desires the fervent love of the hearts of His people.

The account of the failure of Hosea's marriage in the previous three chapters is a parallel of Israel's rebellion against God's covenant love. Hosea's marriage was graciously restored, demonstrating the saving power of God's mercy and love. But it is also used to illustrate the painful consequences of turning away from heartfelt devotion to God. Take for example, Hosea 1:4: "I will put an end to the kingdom of the house of Israel." And Hosea 1:9: "You are not my people, and I am not your God." And Hosea 2:2: "She is not my wife, and I am not her husband." And

Hosea 2:13: "I will punish her for the feast days of the Baals when she … went after her lovers and forgot me, declares the Lord." The message of Hosea's marriage is a clear warning to all God's people that covenant unfaithfulness will result in loss of covenant blessings. The exile in Assyria was a spiritual divorce. When hearts of people are far away from devotion to God, separation from God is the inevitable result.

Hosea's prophetic ministry must have lasted for at least forty years. Chapters 4 through 14 contain a condensed summary of forty years of his preaching to a sinful rebellious nation. Hosea's preaching task was not a pleasant one. Through him God sent one consistent message of a broken marriage covenant, for His people were turning away to other gods. He warned that refusal to acknowledge the true and living God would surely bring severe judgment on the nation. God states the grounds for divorce! Hosea gives the grievous details of Israel's unfaithfulness and lack of love for their God.

Hosea's preaching is not joyful and uplifting! He is very severe, going into great detail as he describes the sin of his nation and the resulting judgment. He uses a vast quantity and variety of poignant verbal images in his attempts to convince the people of their need for repentance. Their refusal to heed his preaching over such a long period of time reveals the intransigence of their hearts hardened against the Lord.

Yet as Hosea's marital disaster ended with the blessing of restoration through amazing love and forgiveness, so Hosea's preaching holds forth the same glorious hope. God's love and promises to his covenant people will endure! While condemning their sin and rebellion, Hosea continually calls them to repentance and promised restoration. Chapters 4 and 5 detail Israel's spiritual adultery in pursuing other gods. But Hosea 6:1–3 is a call to repentance! Chapters 6–10 focus on Israel's covenant transgression.

But Hosea 10:12 is a call to repentance! Chapters 11–13 give a picture of Israel as the prodigal son, turning aside from the rich blessings of God's family and coming to utter ruin. But Hosea 14:1–3 is a call to repentance! And Hosea 14:4–9 gives a glorious promise of healing and restoration. In Hosea 14:4 God's concluding words are: "I will heal their apostasy; I will love them freely, for my anger has turned from them." Rich promises of blessing and fruitfulness follow. God's covenant love endures forever. He will chastise His people for their sins in order to bring about the glorious purpose of His kingdom among them.

God moved Hosea to write down this message for us. To all God's covenant people Hosea proclaims God's grace, in which we may rest and remain in His covenant blessings. Hosea is the prophet of love because He is pointing us to the fullness of God's infinite love made known to the whole world in Jesus Christ.

In the New Testament the apostle of love sets forth the necessity and hope of abiding in covenant love: "And we have seen and testify that the Father has sent his Son to be the Savior of the world. Whoever confesses that Jesus is the Son of God, God abides in him, and he in God. So we have come to know and to believe the love that God has for us. God is love, and whoever abides in love abides in God, and God abides in him" (1 Jn 4:14–16). God's free love is the glue that keeps us abiding in union with Him. Abiding means that we are enabled to rest and remain and continue securely in His promised covenant blessings. Christ, the royal bridegroom calls His church to all the blessings of His love and care as His bride. His love will indeed abide in us and sustain us through all the storms and pitfalls of this life. God's abiding love in Christ will endure all the way to its fulfillment at the glorious marriage supper that will last forever.

When We Hear the Voice of God
Hosea 4:4–9

HOW DO WE react to the voice of God in our daily lives? Do we listen to the voice of the Holy Spirit of God as He speaks to our hearts through the holy scriptures? Surely the whole counsel of God's will for our life and salvation is found in the Bible. There God speaks of the riches of His covenant blessings to us in Christ as He sets forth His gracious gift of salvation and our daily walk in communion with Him. How vital that we "be doers of the word, and not hearers only" (James 1:22)!

God brought the serious accusation against Israel (Hos 4:1–3) of violating their covenant marriage vows. Now, in Hosea 4:4, He warns about their response. Do not contend! Do not accuse! How should we respond when God's word exposes our sin? Do we protest God's right to condemn our sins? Do we act as if our private life is our own affair and is none of God's business? Do we even accuse God of failing to provide for our happiness and sense of fulfillment and defend our searching elsewhere for meaning and blessing? God, the judge of all the earth, knows all our thoughts and deeds, and judges with absolute justice. How essential it is for us to submit in humble repentance when He contends with us.

This sin was even more grievous because Israel, under the covenant given through Moses, was designated as God's priest in the world. God established Israel as a kingdom of priests. (Ex 19:6). Their legacy was to serve as priests of the Lord and ministers of God (Is 61:6), planted by the Lord as oaks of righteousness (Is 61:3) under the reign of Christ, the Lord's anointed one (Is 61:1). God's people are consecrated to serve Him in this world, teaching and leading the peoples of the nations to the worship of the one true God. But now, in Hosea 4:4, God is contending with Israel His priest, and in Hosea 4:6, He rejects them as being His priest because they have rejected the knowledge of Him. Hosea insists that Israel has failed in its priestly calling because of its covenant unfaithfulness. The high and holy calling of the people has been rejected and revoked. Instead of contending for God among the peoples, they were contending against Him!

Hosea continues to show in Hosea 4:5–9 why Israel has no possible grounds for contending with God's accusation. The people had broken the gracious covenant relationship with their God, and the coming national destruction reflected their greater spiritual desolation. Now they stumble by day and by night (Hos 4:5), failing to fulfill their priestly and prophetic duties. In the daylight they commit crimes of open rebellion and in the darkness of ignorance of God they are not able to discern a path of righteousness. Because they have rejected the knowledge of God they have been rejected by Him, and their nation (mother, Hos 4:5) will be destroyed. Because they have forgotten God's law (Hos 4:6), God will withhold His blessing from their descendants. They increased greatly in power and wealth during the reign of Jeroboam (Hos 4:7), but their sins likewise increased. Their pride in all their accomplishments will be shattered and turned into shame. Their sin is their livelihood and sustenance (Hos 4:8). They are continually greedy for unjust gain and exploitation. The corrupt ways of the people (Hos 4:9) have inhibited any priestly service to God in the world. In their unfaithful rebellion they can only expect God's rebuke and punishment. How devastating to contend with God's gracious call in our lives! How vital it is to hear and obey His word, the only sure guide to attaining any sense of security, well-being, and peace.

Christ commits to His people this same holy priestly calling in the present age. Christ has made us to be "a kingdom, priests to His God and Father" (Rev 1:6) and "a royal priesthood" to "proclaim the excellencies of him who called us out of darkness into his marvelous light" (1 Pet 2:9). How precious to us, then, must be every word from His mouth. Our hearts must be quick to hear, believe, and obey all He teaches and commands. Christ has entrusted to His church the glorious task of bringing to a dying world the wondrous message of reconciliation and peace with the living God. How wondrous to us is His voice of grace, by which we may seek fellowship and communion with our redeemer God. How tragic it would be to carelessly ignore or forget His abundant faithfulness and love to us in Christ Jesus. Let us daily submit in our hearts to the voice of God with reverence and awe and seek to serve Him with zeal and great thankfulness.

Worship Matters

Hosea 4:10–19

HOSEA COMES NOW to the central issue in the broken marriage relationship between the people of Israel and their God. He has brought (Hos 4:1) a three-fold charge of no faithfulness, no love, and no knowledge of God. Now he declares that at the heart of this broken relationship is spiritual whoredom in the lives of His covenant people. He began the book by proclaiming his central theme, that "the land commits great whoredom by forsaking the Lord" (Hos 1:2). This charge is now repeated: "They have forsaken the Lord to cherish whoredom" (Hos 4:10), and "A spirit of whoredom has led them astray, and they have left their God to play the whore" (Hos 4:12). Israel has been unfaithful to its covenant marriage vows by turning to worship the gods of the surrounding peoples. And so they have sinned grievously against the grace and kindness of their God.

These verses in chapter 4 indicate that God considers false and unwarranted worship to be spiritual whoredom. God in great mercy and love calls His people into covenant relationship to be

His own precious possession, consecrated only to Himself. He requires that their worship be dedicated to Him alone and that their trust be in Him alone. Giving one's ultimate heart allegiance to someone or something other than the God who claims us as His very own is spiritual adultery. God alone is worthy of all worship and adoration from the depth of our souls. Our worship matters intensely to God.

Israel's false worship began by mixing the worship of the Lord with the manner in which the surrounding peoples worshiped their false gods. They followed the religious customs of the nations around them by sacrificing in worship on high places (Hos 4:13), as if those places were nearer to God. This worship was forbidden to Israel (Dt 12:2–4), because God had said He would dwell among His people. They were to "seek the place that the Lord your God will choose … to put His name and make His habitation there" (Dt 12:5). The true God is not contained in the material creation, but He has graciously chosen to dwell spiritually among His people.

Far worse than the place where they worshiped was what they worshiped. Hosea's summary that "Ephraim is joined to idols" (Hos 4:17), reveals a blatant violation of both the first and second commandment. God's command to all humanity is to have no other gods and to worship no visible representation of any god. Worship offered to pagan idols cannot be pleasing to the one true God. Hosea 4:15 is a warning to avoid the false worship taking place at Gilgal and Beth-aven. Beth-aven ("house of wickedness") is a tragic code name for Bethel ("house of God"). God had appeared to Jacob at Bethel, and he worshiped there (Gen 35:14–15). But Jeroboam, the king of Israel, had set up an idol in the form of a calf at Bethel, proclaiming it to be the god who had brought the Israelites up from Egypt (1 Kings 12:28–29). Gilgal had been a sanctuary of worship for Joshua and Samuel (1 Sam

11:14–15) but now was a center of sinful worship (Amos 4:4). Israel worshiped an idol calf at Samaria (Hos 8:4–6) and kept sacrificing to the Baals (Hos 11:2). Hosea speaks of the evil taking place at Gilgal (Hos 9:15) and at Bethel (Hos 10:15). Their places of worship had become centers of evil.

Even more appalling were the pagan rites that Israel had adopted into their worship. Hosea is very blunt in describing these shameful rituals: "The men themselves go aside with prostitutes and sacrifice with cult prostitutes" (Hos 4:14). Even their daughters were becoming shrine prostitutes (Hos 4:13). The spiritual adultery of worshiping other gods was accompanied by literal adultery in the fertility cult worship of the surrounding peoples.

Clearly the people of Israel were very religious. Worship mattered to them. Their worship had an important place in their lives and culture. But God called their worship whoredom. They were unfaithful to their God and showed no knowledge of Him. Does worship matter to God? It is clear here and throughout the scriptures that our worship matters intensely to God. He sanctifies a people to be His very own possession, so that they should bring glory and honor to Him in all their life and worship. Worship is our first duty in life and our highest privilege. So it is vitally important to worship the true and living God only, and only in a manner pleasing to Him. To worship the gods of the unbelieving world around us, or the gods of our imagination, using whatever rituals seem meaningful to us, is an affront and insult to the God of the Bible. For those called to salvation in Christ, His word and Spirit direct our hearts into worship that is rich fellowship in His love. It is a true blessing, a heavenly joy, the very center of our spiritual life. Our worship matters!

Worship matters so much that it must be done in a manner pleasing to God. Hosea is very clear that not all worship is profitable, and wrongful worship does more harm than good! Israel's wrong worship grew out of a lack of spiritual understanding (Hos 4:11, 14) in hearts that were far from God. They inquired of idols made of wood (Hos 4:12) from which they foolishly sought guidance. So far from drawing near to God, their worship was driving Him away. In Hosea 4:17, Hosea says that because of Ephraim's idols God will "leave him alone." They have left their God (Hos 4:12) and thus it has become an offense to swear by His name (Hos 4:15). Their stubborn hearts (Hos 4:16) resisted following God's revealed will and preferred their own direction. Hosea asks the searching question of how God can feed them (Hos 4:16) if they will not be fed by God? Indeed, they eat and are not satisfied (Hos 4:10); all their efforts lead only to futility, shame (Hos 4:19) and ruin (Hos 4:14). They will be swept away as if enveloped by a strong wind (Hos 4:19).

How hard and futile are the hearts of sinful people apart from the grace of God! How prone we are to "exchange the truth of God for a lie and worship and serve the creature rather than the Creator" (Rom 1:25). How tragic if those called by that wondrous grace should neglect the author of such a great salvation (Heb 2:3). Yet God's grace has revealed His will to feed wayward, stubborn sheep "like lambs in a broad pasture" (Hos 4:16), by the good shepherd who laid down His life for His sheep. He raises us up to a new spiritual life in Christ, with hearts transformed by amazing love, so that we may offer our very lives to Him in worship filled with praise and thanksgiving. Let us seek to present to God our entire being, sanctified by the mercy of Christ, an offering holy and pleasing to God (Rom 12:1), which is our spiritual service of worship. This is worship that truly matters.

They Know Not the Lord

Hosea 5:1–7

THE COURTROOM DRAMA of chapter 4 continues in chapter 5. Both chapters begin with the command to "Hear!" The Lord demands the attention of both ears and heart, not only of the entire nation of Israel but the leadership (the king and priests) in particular.

In chapter 4 the Lord acts as prosecutor, making the case for divorce. Israel is charged with covenant unfaithfulness in worshiping and serving other gods. Now, in chapter 5, the Lord acts as the judge rendering a verdict. First, He recognizes how complete and entire is the revolt of His people (Hos 5:1–7), and then He pronounces a judgment of destruction because of the violation of their covenant marriage commitment (Hos 5:8–15). They have set their affection on false gods and have become a people who "know not the Lord" (Hos 5:4).

The judgment is first of all on the leaders (Hos 5:1) who have ensnared the people by leading them into false worship. Mizpah and Tabor had been places of great victory by Israel's leaders

(Barak at Tabor in Judges 4 and Samuel at Mizpah in 1 Samuel 7.) Now their leaders, so far from bringing deliverance at the hand of the Lord, were bringing the nation into bondage through revolt against the Lord. Chapter 4 made clear that their worship entailed sacrifice to pagan idols (Hos 4:13, 14, 17). This unfaithfulness to the Lord their God is called spiritual whoredom. The slaughter (Hos 5:2) may be of literal herds of animals offered in sacrifice, or the spiritual death of the people engaged in rebellious worship. Their princes and priests have ensnared the nation in worship that led them away from the Lord. Now He must discipline them because of their spiritual whoredom.

God views their revolt against Him not only as great injustice but as a broken covenant relationship. God speaks as judge but also as an offended husband. God knows the people, but they no longer know Him. God knows Ephraim (Hos 5:3). He is entirely acquainted with all their ways; their sins are not hidden from the Lord. But a spirit of whoredom dominates their inner being, and consequently they no longer know the Lord (Hos 5:4). They have broken fellowship with their God and their whoredom defiles them. The love essential in their covenant marriage relationship has been given to another. Their hearts are in love with their sin and thus they are not willing to return to the God who has called them to Himself.

Hosea now sets forth the dire consequences of rejecting the knowledge of the true and living God (Hos 5:5–7). God declares that Israel will stumble in their guilt (Hos 5:5) and their covenant unfaithfulness will lead to their downfall. Because they broke faith with the Lord, He has withdrawn from them (Hos 5:6). They will seek Him with an abundance of animal sacrifices, but they will not find Him. Their children are like aliens, refusing to live under the dominion of the Lord. The new moon festivals were celebrated to the gods of pagan fertility cults, with the intention of bringing forth abundance from the earth. But God says these idolatrous celebrations will instead bring only judgment on the crops of their fields (Hos 5:7). The reign of Jeroboam was a time of great power and prosperity for Israel. But the pride of their accomplishments will testify against them (Hos 5:5) because they were done not in dependence but in rebellion against the Lord. They will not enjoy the fruit of their prosperity, but it will testify to their covenant unfaithfulness.

What a dreadful statement of the spiritual state of the people, that when they go to seek the Lord they will not find Him (Hos 5:6). How can this be, that all their religious observance and activity fails to bring them close to the living God? Clearly it was not the Lord they were worshiping but gods of the surrounding culture, the gods of what they could see and touch, the gods of personal comfort and prosperity. They did not even know the Lord (Hos 5:4); their religion defiled them (Hos 5:3) and prevented them from returning to the Lord. What a severe judgment on all manmade religion and on all our devotion to the idols that grow out of the desires of our heart. Worship of created things rather than the Creator does not lead us to know the one true God.

So is it really possible for us to know God? The New Testament definitely gives us a positive answer to this all-important question. Jesus boldly assures us that by our faith in Him we are indeed able to know the Lord! He announces the blessings of a restored relationship with the true and living God in John 10:14–15: "I am the good shepherd. I know my own and my own know me, just as the Father knows me and I know the Father; and I lay down my life for the sheep." The extraordinary truth is that our union and fellowship with Christ is of the same essential nature as that of the Son of God with His heavenly Father! Jesus said, "If you had known me, you would have known my Father also. From now on you do know Him and have seen Him" (Jn 14:7). We may know the true God but only because in infinite grace and mercy, the good shepherd calls His own to Himself, having first laid down His life for them.

How can we come to know the Lord? His sheep hear His voice and follow Him (Jn 10:27). We must hear the voice of the Lord Jesus, believe it, submit to it, and follow His every word. We submit to His absolute claim on our lives to be our Savior and our King. Our relationship with Him can only begin with hearts overwhelmed by God's powerful kindness and mercy revealed in our Lord Jesus Christ. We follow Him as we bow in humble submission to His rule over our lives, depending on His glorious grace to lead us into living in obedience to His will.

To know Him means to worship Him for who He is, the eternal God and Lord of the universe. It is to acknowledge His rightful ownership of our entire being as our Creator and Redeemer. We confess that He alone is our life, our hope, our peace, and our King. We give Him back the life He has given us. We love Him by living in light of His love, in which He gave Himself for us even to death. Walking with Him, we know his presence to guide the steps of our lives and to bring comfort and peace in all circumstances. Then our lives are filled with rejoicing in the Lord, knowing His deliverance from the power of evil and the glorious certain hope of life forever in His kingdom.

Seek the Lord

Hosea 5:8–15

THE PURPOSE OF the book of Hosea is to convince us that God's mercy in the covenant of grace triumphs over the wicked rebellion of His people. This display of God's covenant love for sinners is so unexpected and radical that Hosea repeats it in various ways through fourteen chapters. The last verse of chapter 5 is one of Hosea's boldly profound statements of God's redeeming love.

The Lord's nation had tragically departed from Him, and now His prophet announces impending utter devastation as previously declared in Hosea 1:4-5. And yet the purpose of God even here is still gracious to His covenant people, as becomes clear in Hosea 5:15. His desire is that in their distress they will acknowledge their guilt and then return to their God and earnestly seek Him. God has a gracious purpose, even in pronouncing judgment on His wayward nation. His desire is not to destroy but to bring about repentance and restoration of covenant blessing to His people, and through them to the whole world. His message is that God's powerful grace overcomes our sinful guilt. He calls us to seek Him from the heart.

In Hosea 5:8 the sound of the horn and trumpet is a warning of an invading force and a call to prepare for war. "We follow you, O Benjamin!" is a battle cry taken from a previous battle in Judges 5:14. In Hosea 5:9–11 the danger is stated clearly, as "desolation in the day of punishment" and being "crushed in judgment." Although He employs a foreign army, it is the Lord who makes known what is sure (Hos 5:9) and pours out His wrath like a flood (Hos 5:10). The Lord's hand has turned against His nation.

It is significant that the threat and warning is given not only to the northern kingdom of Ephraim but also to the southern kingdom of Judah. In Hosea 4:15 there is a warning to Judah not to engage in the guilt of the rebellious kingdom of Israel. Now, in Hosea 5:5, 12, 13, and 14, Judah is mentioned as bearing the same sins and judgment as Ephraim. In Hosea 5:8, Gibeah and Ramah were cities in the territory of the tribe of Benjamin, and Benjamin, located between the two kingdoms, had remained loyal to Judah. The mention in Hosea 5:9 of "the tribes of Israel" appears to indicate all twelve tribes, meaning that both kingdoms now had become unfaithful to the Lord's covenant grace. "Bad company ruins good morals" (1 Cor 15:33). Israel's sin of idolatry spread like a contagious disease.

So where will Israel turn for help in the face of this great danger? The fearful reality stated in Hosea 5:12 is that as they have abandoned the Lord, they will find no help from Him. Rather, He will be a destructive force, like a moth and dry rot to them. The picture is of small, barely perceptible enemies that gradually over time work great devastation. God will secretly remove all Israel's strength, all they have relied upon.

Their next attempt was to look to earthly powers for help. Ironically they turned to the king of Assyria (Hos 5:13), the world superpower of that day, which would eventually be the source of their total destruction. But they found that no earthly king was able to cure or heal them, because their sickness was spiritual and their wound was by decree of the Lord. Spiritual healing could only be found by returning in their hearts to the Lord and seeking restoration by His grace and mercy.

But because their hearts remained hardened in devotion to other gods, the Lord was instead revealed as a lion (Hos 5:14) to them. His sovereign power prevails to capture and destroy His enemies; no one can stand against Him. His promise to tear and go away and carry off is a clear picture of the Assyrian invasion and exile of Israel. The awesome military power of Assyria was a reminder of the far greater dominion of the Lord, which no one was able to rescue from His hand.

In Hosea 5:15, the lion will return to His place, leaving total destruction. God will withdraw from His people, as previously stated in Hosea 5:6, and they will not find Him. But this lion has a gracious purpose not only to destroy but also to restore. His desired end is that they would acknowledge their guilt, repent of their sin, and seek His face. So He will be graciously active even in their great distress, until they turn away from their sin and seek Him in true worship. God is a merciful lion, always calling us to return to the Lord, our rightful husband, even as Hosea had brought his wayward wife, Gomer, back into his love and care.

God has indeed withdrawn from all who love sin and persist in it, but for those who truly seek Him He holds forth a glorious hope of restoration. Hosea 5:15 is a rich promise for rebellious sinners. In their distress they are to earnestly seek Him. They are to acknowledge their guilt and seek God's face. They will find pardoning grace and spiritual union with the living God.

Seeking the Lord means first of all acknowledging our guilt and crying out to Him for mercy and forgiveness. Secondly, it means calling upon Him in worship, humbly bowing before His glory and might, and submitting to His sovereign rule over our life. Third, it means communion with Him in prayer, expressing our utter dependence upon Him for all that is good and right. And it means earnestly striving to live in obedience to His commands. It means turning away from all that is displeasing to Him and submitting to His authority to rule over every aspect of life and every desire of our heart. By definition we must seek the Lord with a fervent desire from the depth of our being, not merely an external show.

Seeking the Lord is our response to the working of God's grace in our lives, for He desires to be found by us. He promises that all who seek Him will find (Mt 7:7) and He rewards those who earnestly seek Him (Heb 11:6). In this grace we are given strong encouragement in scripture: "Seek the Lord while He may be found; call upon Him while He is near; let the wicked forsake his way, and the unrighteous man his thoughts; let him return to the Lord, that He may have compassion on him, and to our God, for He will abundantly pardon" (Is 55:6–7). "You will seek me and find me, when you seek me with all your heart. I will be found by you …" (Jer 29:13–14). Incredibly, God Himself is seeking union and communion with His people: "… the true worshipers will worship the Father in spirit and truth, for the Father is seeking such people to worship Him" (Jn 4:23). "For the Son of Man came to seek and save the lost" (Lk 19:10). Thanks be eternally to our Lord Jesus Christ, who seeks us first so that we may also seek Him and receive eternal blessing from His gracious hand.

Call to Repentance
Hosea 6:1–3

IN THE PREVIOUS two chapters Hosea has made an overwhelming case for the guilt and unfaithfulness of the people and warned of the impending judgment that would certainly result. Now he proclaims amazing deliverance from the coming wrath through God's merciful command of repentance. The glorious, good news is that God is not seeking to destroy His people but to restore them to Himself.

"Come let us return to the Lord" (Hos 6:1) is God's urgent message of repentance, spoken through His prophet. This is a desperately needed word of great hope! Hosea's purpose was that the people would be heartbroken because of the calamity of their sin. Now he directs that instead of despairing over their perilous situation, they must seek forgiveness and deliverance in the wondrous mercy of our God.

Hosea's words first proclaim forgiveness! This call to repentance demonstrates God's amazing covenant mercy for rebellious sinners. Despite their unfaithfulness, He has not given up on His people or abandoned them. Rather, He seeks to restore to them all the blessings of His covenant.

God's call is really His command, expressing His will for His people to return to Him and find forgiveness. As they have forsaken their God and turned away from Him, so now Hosea proclaims the pathway to return to the Lord. The way of restoration begins with humility, by acknowledging their guilt (Hos 5:15) and turning away from all that is displeasing to Him. Humbling themselves before His mighty power, (the lion, Hos 5:14) they must earnestly seek Him. Normally, of course, we would attempt to hide ourselves from the lion who threatened to tear us apart. The astonishing feature in this call is that, instead of seeking to escape from the lion, we return to Him and find His mercy and forgiveness.

The prophet includes himself ("let us return") in this call to repent of corporate sins. These were the sins of the nation, and Hosea leads the people in corporate repentance. The godly leaders in the Old Testament whom God often employed to call the people back to Himself were sinners like ourselves, and they knew they were also debtors to God's mercy. So they included themselves in humbling and confessing the guilt of the people (see Daniel 9 and Ezra 9), because they had found God's forgiveness and cleansing power in their own lives. How amazing is the compassionate love of our God in restoring sinners to Himself!

Secondly, Hosea proclaims radical healing and transformation. God in mercy shows forth His power to heal and bind up our sin-inflicted wounds (Hos 6:1). God is able to reverse the effects of sin in our lives, He can undo the consequences of our errors, and He can turn our tears into joy. The nation had already been sorely wounded and afflicted (Hos 5:13), with promise of more severe tearing to come (Hos 5:14). But this affliction was a chastisement, with the intent of leading the nation back to fellowship with their God if only they would repent of their idolatry. In God's mercy His chastisement lasts only for a short time (two or three days, Hos 6:2) and works not to destroy but to restore His people. Only God's grace and mercy have the power to transform sinful rebellious hearts into living trophies of love and thankfulness to Him.

God's call to repentance proclaims new life! The words of Hosea 6:2 speak of "reviving us" and "raising us up," a glorious picture of life from the dead. The result of raising up His people is "that we may live before Him" (Hos 6:2). God gives the promise that those who are dead in their sins will be raised up to enjoy a renewed relationship with Himself. This promise is fulfilled in Christ, who was raised from the dead on the third day. In Christ we "were also raised with him through faith in the powerful working of God, who raised Him from the dead. And you (we) … God made alive together with Him, having forgiven all our trespasses …" (Col 2:12–13). Surely "living before Him" must mean a commitment to reject sinful ways and live in obedience to His commands. All our life is to be lived in His presence, all our being must be consecrated to Him, and all our activity presented as an offering of worship to Him. God's call to return to Him is a matter of our hearts made alive by His spirit, that His word and will may have first priority in our lives.

Hosea's call proclaims friendship with God! The exhortation to "press on to know the Lord' (Hos 6:3) confirms the reality of a restored relationship with the God who created us. It speaks of strong desire and diligent pursuit of something very precious and important. What could be more precious than finding reconciliation and peace with God our Creator? We are brought into communion with the living God and assured of His powerful working in the details of our life. In fellowship with Him we seek to know and do His will, trust Him for all we need, and walk in the blessed light of His love. His call to repentance is a call to God-centered living.

God's call to repentance brings us great assurance! In Hosea 6:3, "His going out is sure as the dawn." As sure as the night will be replaced by daylight, so sure it is that God like a workman will go forth in the new day to work His grace into the lives of His people. He will certainly come to those who seek Him; they will find Him and receive from Him great blessing.

Finally, His call brings rich blessings! God's presence with us is like the spring rains (Hos 6:3) that water the earth, bringing forth life and fruitfulness. His coming is like a river of living water by the Holy Spirit, who dwells with us and in us (Jn 7:39). The Spirit of Christ in us is the source and power of true spiritual life in union with the living God. He brings forth the spiritual fruit of righteousness, peace, and joy in the kingdom of God. Through His power our lives are transformed to serve Him in this world and bring glory to His name. Such is His purpose and will in bringing sinful men and women to repentance and faith by His healing mercy.

For indeed Christ has come to us, that in Him all humankind may return to the Lord. God's presence has come among us in Christ, the sun of righteousness who has risen upon us with healing in his wings (Mal 4:2). Hosea's call to return to the Lord was a call to embrace again the promise of the Messiah! Christ gives us the same call and promise: "Come to me, all who labor and are heavy laden, and I will give you rest" (Mt 11:28). He alone comes with power and grace to provide for sinners forgiveness and the gift of new spiritual life. In Christ alone is shown the mercy of the Lord with power to save sinners from eternal condemnation and bring them safely into all the glories of the kingdom of God. Come, let us return to the Lord in the grace of Christ!

Vanishing Love

Hosea 6:4–6

WHAT WAS ISRAEL'S response to God's call to repentance in Hosea 6:1–3? This gracious invitation was entirely ignored! Chapters 6–10 of Hosea's prophecy continue to severely rebuke Israel for the same sins condemned in chapters 4 and 5. Hosea 6:6–7 contains the same indictment as Hosea 4:1: that of no faithfulness, no love, and no knowledge of God.

We must note the tragic rejection of God's gracious call to reconciliation in the verses soon following:

> Come, let us return to the Lord (Hos 6:1), but they do not return or seek Him (Hos 7:10).

> He will heal us (Hos 6:1), but when He would heal them, their sin vividly shows forth (Hos 7:1).

> He will raise us up that we may live before Him (Hos 6:2), but they have strayed from Him (Hos 7:13).

Let us press on to know the Lord (Hos 6:3), but none of them calls on Him (Hos 7:7).

His going out is sure as the dawn (Hos 6:3), but they have dealt faithlessly with Him (Hos 6:7).

No wonder God cries out to them, "What shall I do with you?" (Hos 6:4). Their response to His love is to run in the opposite direction!

For their love for Him had vanished (Hos 6:4) like the morning clouds or dew that disappears in the heat of the day. The people God had called to Himself to be His chosen possession had initially committed to follow His command to "Love the Lord your God with all your heart and with all your soul and with all your might" (Dt 6:5). But their love had not continued. The pressures of life in this world and the lure of imitating the cultures around them had led them away from obedience to the commands of the Lord. They abandoned their first love (Rev 2:4), even setting their hearts on serving and depending on other gods. Their love had not endured but had quickly vanished away in the trials of ordinary life.

Do we ever wonder what it is God desires most of all from us? He leaves us no doubt in Hosea 6:6. "I desire steadfast love and not sacrifice, the knowledge of God rather than burnt offerings." God wants first of all our hearts to be on fire with love for Him, living in intimate communion and devotion to Him. And He has done all that is necessary to accomplish His desire in our lives! He has first shown to us His extraordinary redeeming love, which transforms our lives into strongholds of love for Him. He not only tells us of His love but demonstrates it visibly, revealing Himself to us so that we may know Him. He has demonstrated the greatest love the world has ever known in Christ, who gave Himself even to death, to bring about reconciliation with those who were His enemies. In Christ, God has "stooped to ask of us the love of our poor hearts" (adapted from Frederick W. Faber's hymn, "My God How Wonderful Thou Art"). It is only to our shame and disgrace if we fail to acknowledge the infinite riches of His love. Our love for Him, in response to His far greater love for us, must be the vital impulse of our life and existence.

The priority of this kind of love is clearly revealed in the life and words of Jesus. Matthew's gospel records two occasions where Jesus quotes from Hosea 6:6. "I desire mercy and not sacrifice" (Mt 9:13 and 12:7). On both occasions the Pharisees were critical of Jesus's mercy to those in need, because it was not in accord with their understanding of the requirements of God's law. They did not regard those to whom Jesus showed love as being worthy of love. Their worship consisted of outward ritual, with little effect on their hearts and lives. Jesus makes it clear that mercy is at the very heart of His ministry to sinners in this world. "I came not to call the righteous, but sinners" (Mt 9:13). We can only show that we understand the power of His amazing love for sinners if we in turn imitate His love in acts of kindness toward others. The only acceptable worship arises out of hearts overflowing with God's infinite love. The essence of His kingdom is mercy and forgiveness.

But God did require the sacrifices and burnt offerings of the Old Testament church. Why did He command them to be offered? The sacrifices the people of God offered in worship were meant to show their love, devotion, and dependent trust in their God. To offer sacrifice without hearts of love is a contradiction. To bring ritual worship from lives filled with unrepentant sin is an abomination. This is explained in Psalm 50, where God calls His covenant people (Ps 50:4–5) to testify against them (Ps 50:7)! His rebuke is not because of their sacrifices (Ps 50:8), although He has no need of them (Ps 50:9–13), but for their wicked, godless lifestyle (Ps 50:16–22), which denied the sincerity of their worship. He commands offerings from hearts possessed of thanksgiving and devoted trust (Ps 50:14, 23). This is worship that truly brings glory and honor to the most high God.

What if our love for Him becomes lifeless and cold? God often uses drastic means to cause our vanished love to return. God sent prophets and preachers (Hos 6:5) with severe warnings. The Old Testament's prophetic books are filled with repeated condemnation of our sins. God's prophets have "hewn" our thoughtless lifestyle and "slain" our rebellious nature. How prone we are to wander and forget the steadfast love of the Lord! God knows we need this continual reminder to walk in a manner worthy of our calling. God says His "judgment goes forth as the light" (Hos 6:5). His judgments come not only in words but also are visible in circumstances of life. Numerous Old Testament events are set forth as chastisements because of the sinful rebellion of God's people. His judgments go forth as a bright light, exposing sin and revealing all that is hidden in darkness. It may be that when His love is withdrawn from us, we will notice that we have lost a precious and wonderful thing and will seek His love again. His purpose is to restore and renew our hearts to fervent, devoted, lifelong love.

"Give thanks to the Lord for He is good, for His steadfast love endures forever" (Ps 136:1). His love for His covenant people never fails or vanishes, "but the steadfast love of the Lord is from everlasting to everlasting on those who fear Him" (Ps 103:17). How weak is our love for Him by comparison, and yet He is gracious to receive and sanctify our meager love when we come to Him with humble, thankful hearts. Let us renew our love for Him each day, let us nurture our love in the truth of His Word, and let us rely on His grace to cause our love to grow. Let us serve Him faithfully, with hearts rooted and grounded in His love. May our love for our Savior never be diminished but continue to increase and bear fruit for eternal glory. "Grace to all who love our Lord Jesus Christ with an undying love" (Eph 6:24, NIV).

Transgressed My Covenant

Hosea 6:7

"THEY HAVE TRANSGRESSED my covenant" (Hos 6:7, 8:1). This simple statement serves as a comprehensive and devastating assessment of the deplorable spiritual condition of the kingdom of Israel during the final forty years leading up to its ultimate destruction in 722 BC. The central theme of chapters 6 through 10 of Hosea's prophecy is the covenant unfaithfulness of God's people and its shattering effect on the nation.

God's covenants in scripture describe the structure of His gracious dealings with humanity. His covenant expresses His commitment to be the blessing and reward for a people chosen in His love. God entered into a covenant bond with Israel to show forth His sovereign calling, provision, and protection of those He set apart as His own. As He pledged to be faithful to His promises to His people, so they were to faithfully continue in obedience and dependence on Him. To transgress His covenant means to rebel against His sovereign rule and reject His gracious union with His people. Hosea 1:9 sums up the tragic consequence of covenant transgression: "You are not my people, and I am not your God."

God states, "Like Adam they have transgressed the covenant" (Hos 6:7). God had entered into a covenant of creation with Adam. The requirement of perfect obedience to one command (not to eat of the forbidden fruit) represented a commitment of loyalty to the absolute rule of God. God's pledge of communion and blessing to Adam was portrayed in the abundant provision of the garden of Eden. The covenant contained the promise of continued blessing and fellowship with God resulting from obedience, but also warned of spiritual separation and death as the consequence of disobedience. Israel's covenant transgression was essentially the same as Adam's disobedience. Both were unfaithful to God's sovereign rule; both rejected communion with God and His unlimited blessings. Israel's people, like Adam, had declared independence from God and claimed absolute control over their existence. But independence from God means isolation from God and from all His blessings.

The same accusation is repeated in Hosea 8:1, where transgression of God's covenant is coupled with rebellion against God's law. The covenant God made with Israel through Moses revealed His faithfulness and steadfast love for His people (Dt 7:9). They in turn were to be committed to show their devotion to the one true God by keeping all His commandments (Dt 4:13; Ex 24:7). This covenant centered on God's law, by which He directed the people to be separate from the world, a nation set apart for God's service. The people rightly pledged to live by God's laws but tragically failed to persevere in following them. Rebellion against God's revealed will signaled disregard for the God who had established the covenant.

This theme of covenant unfaithfulness continues the theme of broken marriage in Hosea's prophecy. Scripture speaks of the marriage relationship as a covenant (Mal 2:14; Prov 2:17). Hosea's broken marriage (chapters 1–3) is a picture of Israel's marital unfaithfulness to her God, and God's suit of divorce (chapters 4 and 5) represents God's righteous judgment on those who have turned away from His love. Hosea wants to make clear that the rejection of God's gracious covenant commitment is even more heinous than the destruction of a marriage relationship.

Moses in Deuteronomy 28 sets forth delightful covenant blessings that accompany the keeping of God's commands but a much longer listing of covenant curses for disobedience. Hosea in chapters 6–10 repeats many of these curses, fulfilling in his day the chastisement promised for covenant disobedience. First he describes the intensity of their evil deeds, their rebellion against the Lord, and their idolatry (chapters 7 and 8). Then he speaks of the futility in all their endeavors, the failure of their worship, their lack of fruitfulness, the threat of foreign invasion, and the termination of their kingdom (chapters 9 and 10). Covenant blessings cannot continue apart from persevering covenant faithfulness to our God.

The prophet Jeremiah, writing more than one hundred years after Hosea, looks back at Israel's failure to persevere in God's covenant. In Jeremiah 31:32 he speaks of "my covenant that they broke, though I was their husband, declares the Lord." And like Hosea, he proclaims the hope of future glorious blessing through God's covenant faithfulness. He promises a new covenant (Jer 31:31), not like the covenant made through Moses but one based on better promises. These promises are contained in several "I will" statements (Jer 31:33–34), emphasizing that it is the working of God's grace that fulfills His covenant purpose in His people. This new covenant is not like the covenant made through Moses (Jer 31:32), because now Christ has accomplished all that is needed for us to enter and persevere in His covenant grace forever. Christ is the mediator of this new covenant (Heb 9:15), because by His death He purchased our promised eternal inheritance.

The new covenant is an unbreakable covenant. Christ has purchased our covenant perseverance! Jesus spoke of this at the Last Supper: "This cup that is poured out for you is the new covenant in my blood" (Lk 22:20). The life of the Son of God poured out for us is the guarantee of the covenant. How could there possibly be a greater or more precious pledge of assurance of all God's blessings to His people? For Christ gave Himself for the forgiveness of our sins. By faith we are united to Him, and through Him we know the true and living God. His law is no longer merely written on our doorposts but now is written on our hearts and commands our will. We are saved by God's grace revealed in Christ's death and resurrection and we persevere in salvation by that same grace.

Because Christ has accomplished all that is necessary for our eternal salvation, He powerfully fulfills all God's covenant promises for His people. The gracious work He has begun in His children will last to eternity. "For by a single offering he has perfected for all time those who are being sanctified" (Heb 10:14). His gift to us is the grace to persevere in His steadfast love to the end. The promise of His covenant is unbreakable, because Christ has accomplished our salvation from first to last.

I Have Seen a Horrible Thing

Hosea 6:8–7:7

COVENANT-BREAKING IS SURE to result in serious sinning. God's prophet here lists a whole catalog of heinous crimes that had become manifest as Israel sank into social disorder. Murder and whoredom become commonplace. Thieves break in and bandits raid outside. Evil deeds and anarchy are predominant. The priests band together for robbery, and the kings and princes rejoice in evil and make a mockery of justice. These would indeed be dark days of decline for any people. God's covenant with Israel required the keeping of His commandments. Such rampant wickedness can only indicate a spiritual decay and rejection of the gracious God of the covenant.

Hosea is intent on reminding his people that the God they have rejected is still present and watching all their sin. God speaks through the prophet: "In the house of Israel I have seen a horrible thing" (Hos 6:10). "I remember all their evil. Their deeds … are before my face" (Hos 7:2). When the Lord draws near to heal and restore His people, the light of His holiness uncovers all their evil deeds (Hos 7:1). Although His words focus mainly on Israel, he also finds a similar condition in Judah. He sends to Judah the warning that "a harvest is appointed" (Hos 6:11). They will reap what they sow, and God will repay in His appointed time. We need this reminder that our sins cannot be concealed from God's sight. "No creature is hidden from his sight, but all are naked and exposed to the eyes of him to whom we must give account" (Heb 4:13)

Hosea gives a devastating picture of the leadership of the nation in Hosea 7:4–7. During the last thirty years of Israel's history, according to 2 Kings 15 and 17, there were six kings who all did evil in God's sight. Three of them reigned for two years or less, four were assassinated, and the last one taken prisoner to Assyria. Hosea here vividly describes this period of descent into chaos and anarchy. According to Hosea, the kings themselves rejoiced in evil (Hos 7:3), surrounded themselves with mockers (Hos 7:5), and did not call on the Lord (Hos 7:7). The government officials (princes) engaged in the wildest sinful carousing while plotting treachery and intrigue against each other. Hosea likens them to a heated oven, slowly growing in the heat of anger and malice, then blazing forth in uncontrollable rage to destroy and devour their rulers. Such "horrible things" could not long endure among the people whom the Lord had called by His name. He had ordained to show forth through them His powerful grace and sovereign rule over the earth. But instead they were ignoring His rule and imitating the sins of the surrounding nations.

Do we in Christ's church today have this same tragic tendency to so quickly return to our former ungodly patterns of behavior and to the lifestyles of this world? How horrible all our sins are, especially in light of His grace and kindness to us in our Lord Jesus Christ. Can we live in the glorious blessing of steadfast covenant faithfulness purchased for us by our Savior? Only by trusting in the redeeming grace of Christ do we find power to persevere in His covenant blessings.

We are made into new creations in Christ, and He has delivered us from the dominion of sin. We have been taught by our Lord Jesus "to put off your old self, which belongs to your former manner of life … and to put on the new self, created after the likeness of God in true righteousness, and holiness" (Eph 4:20–24). His will for us is to be holy, consecrated to Himself. What He commands He also now gives us grace to fulfill. He sends forth His mighty spirit, who is able to transform our lowly lives into beautiful treasures for Him.

The voice of the Lord Jesus still speaks: "If you love me you will keep my commandments" (Jn 14:15). Christ has loved us first, and that love gives us new hearts that can both love Him and keep His commands. Let us diligently seek to show forth our love with the good fruit of lives renewed by His grace and be eager to do all His holy will.

They Rebel against Me
Hosea 7:8–16

IN CHAPTER 6, Hosea complains that the people of his nation have no love but only covenant transgression. Then he says they have no justice but only horrible crimes. Now he continues to say that they have no integrity but only rebellion.

Covenant transgression consists of rebellion against our God. Hosea says: "They have strayed from me … They have rebelled against me … They speak lies against me … they do not cry to me from the heart…they have departed from me…they devise evil against me" (Hos 7:13–15). The people of Israel were living in direct rejection and opposition to the God who, in great covenant love, had brought them out of bondage to be a people for His very own. How could this be?

This was a spiritual rebellion, but it was made manifest in the political life of the nation. Hosea states the heart of the matter in Hosea 7:8: "Ephraim mixes himself with the peoples." In Exodus 34:10–16, the Lord speaks of His covenant that separated Israel from the surrounding nations. He pledges to drive out the inhabitants of the promised land and warns Israel not to enter into a covenant of peace with them. He proclaims judgment on the gods of those nations, commanding Israel to destroy the altars and objects of worship in the land. He separates His people from the nations in order to prevent the worship of their false gods. He declares that He will do marvels not seen in any other nation (Ex 34:10) and the peoples around them will see the awesome work of God for Israel. Set apart as the people belonging to the Lord, Israel was to show forth among the nations of the world the glory and power of the one true God. Mixed with the nations, in disobedience to God's command, Israel had descended into idolatrous worship and rejection of their covenant God.

Hosea uses some poignant metaphors to describe Israel's wretched condition. "Ephraim is a cake not turned" (Hos 7:8), burned on one side, uncooked and doughy on the other. In seeking to follow the ways and customs of pagan peoples, Israel had neglected its own good and lost all integrity as the people chosen by God. Failing to fulfill their own potential for goodness, they had become something useless, unpalatable. They had grown old before their time and their strength was consumed by another (Hos 7:9). But they did not notice, because in their pride they believed all would be well. To the contrary, it was their self-sufficient pride and their refusal to repent that testified against them (Hos 7:10), because they relied on the powers of this world instead of seeking help from the Lord.

Hosea 7:11 compares them to a silly dove without sense. Weak, vulnerable, and without direction, they flutter off first to Egypt and then to Assyria, seeking security. God says He will capture them and bring them down (Hos 7:12), which is the discipline He had promised in the Law of Moses and the prophets ("the report made to the congregation" [Hos 7:12].) This promise is a picture of the coming exile, where Israel's freedom would end in captivity under the very kingdoms where they had sought help. Hosea 7:13 pronounces "Woe to them ... destruction to them" because their spiritual decay is about to become a national disaster. Their rebellion has left them with no vitality, no integrity, no strength.

And still our gracious God reaches out to them in mercy and kindness. He would redeem them (Hos 7:13), but they speak lies about His ability or willingness to act for them. He would provide for all their needs if they cried out to Him from their hearts (Hos 7:14). Instead they mourn over their losses and call on the pagan gods of the nations. They even gash themselves, shedding their own blood to entreat the attention of those gods, like the prophets of Baal on Mount Carmel (1 Kings 18:28). He had trained and strengthened their arms (Hos 7:15), which they now were raising in rebellion against Him. He reminds them of His faithful care and provision for them, if they continue in faithfulness to Him alone as their sovereign Lord.

But their thoughts and steps are not upward (Hos 7:16) toward the living and true God. Like a faulty bow, they fall short and miss the mark, far from God, useless for any good. They speak insolent words toward God, but Egypt, from where they escaped out of bondage, will speak insulting words toward them.

How can we overcome the natural rebellion of our hearts and live in righteousness and integrity before God? Christ has redeemed us from the heart rebellion of our sinful condition. "He himself bore our sins in his body on the tree, that we might die to sin and live to righteousness. By his wounds you have been healed. For you were straying like sheep, but have now returned to the Shepherd and Overseer of your souls" (1 Pet 2:24–25). Christ's giving Himself over to death in our place, bearing in His body the awful wrath of God for our sins, is for our healing and life and righteousness. How wondrously does this gift of love completely provide for our spiritual life and vitality! Our straying hearts are captured and healed under the relentless pursuit of the good shepherd. Through faith in Christ we are enabled to submit to and delight in His watchful care over our souls.

Let us return to Him again and again to find forgiveness and healing for all our wanderings. When we are tempted to reject God's good gifts to us and look to the surrounding world for our help and direction, let us remember the body of Christ offered up for us in His unlimited love. By His redeeming power, all those who are united to Christ through faith are given grace to partake in His dying to sin (Rom 6:10–11). Made alive with Christ, we are enabled to put off the rebellion of our hearts and live increasingly in His righteousness. Christ's mercy is sufficient for us. He will lead us faithfully through this fallen world to share in His eternal glory.

When We Don't Know That We Don't Know

Hosea 8:1–6

CHAPTER 8 BEGINS with an ominous warning: "Set the trumpet to your lips!" (Hos 8:1). Here is a shout giving warning of military invasion. The eagle (Hos 8:1) signifies an enemy of terrifying power, ready to suddenly swoop down and carry off its prey. The house of the Lord is not the temple in Jerusalem but the household, the people God had called by His name. Clearly this is a dire warning of impending doom upon the northern kingdom of Israel.

The reason for such severe judgment is also stated in Hosea 8:1: "because they have transgressed my covenant and rebelled against my law." They have broken the vows of their marriage covenant with the Lord and rebelled against His holy kingship. They are no longer His people and He is not their God (Hos 1:9). He will pursue divorce from this broken relationship of unfaithfulness and disdained love by sending the people into exile.

Hosea had already brought the accusation of transgressing of God's covenant (Hos 6:7). Chapters 6 and 7 follow with a description of resulting crimes, anarchy, and rebellion. In those chapters Hosea charges the people with having no love, no covenant-keeping, no justice, and no integrity. Now he adds the serious accusation that they have no knowledge of God (as in Hosea 4:1) but have provoked God's anger by worshiping idols. In chapters 8–10, Hosea's preaching contains a lengthy description of the severe judgments soon to come on the nation of Israel because of the people's rejection of the covenant love of God.

But while Hosea proclaims God's righteous judgment, he also appeals to the people to come to their senses and return to their God. Hosea presents us with a summary of forty years of his preaching to God's congregation while being ignored by the vast majority. Yet God is patient and merciful with erring people, always compassionately calling them back to Himself. Sinful men and women are never able to keep the requirements of God's covenant. Yet Hosea is pointing us to the covenant in which God graciously fulfills for us in Christ all that is needed for our eternal union and communion with the living God.

Israel protests God's judgment. They cry out to Him: "My God, we—Israel—know you" (Hos 8:2). But God's answer in Hosea 8:3 is very clear: They have rejected what is good. As they have pursued that which is at enmity to God, so shall an enemy pursue them.

Had Israel really rejected their highest good and greatest blessing? They address Him as "My God." But is it really Him they are seeking to love and serve? Are they making a heart commitment to submit to His sovereign power and present their lives in worship to Him alone? They claim to know Him, but are they seeking to live their daily lives in intimate personal communion with their redeemer God?

It is entirely possible that we may be so deluded that we don't know that we don't know God. Tragically, there are many who call God their friend and yet ignore His commands (Mt 7:21). We may think it is all well and good in our relationship with our Creator, and yet be living in rebellion against the truth He has revealed in His word. Jesus spoke of those who honor God with their lips, while their hearts are far from Him, worshiping Him in vain (Mt 15:8–9). If we have truly come to know God, will not the evidence of a transformed life be readily apparent? One who knows God must bow before His sovereign rule in total dependence on His grace and power, to joyfully honor and serve Him with their whole being.

Hosea now presents strong evidence to justify this charge that, so far from knowing God, Israel has spurned all His good blessings to them. They have chosen their leaders (Hos 8:4) without His help, rejecting His rule as their ultimate Lord and King. Far worse, they have used their prosperity to create false gods (Hos 8:4–6), which will not lead to their deliverance but rather their destruction. Their idols will incur God's wrath and rejection. God declares that people who worship such idols are incapable of innocence (Hos 8:5). Israel has also turned to other nations and hired them as lovers (Hos 8:9), placing in people of this world the hope and trust that ought to belong to God alone. They have regarded His law as a strange thing (Hos 8:12), relying on their own wisdom to direct their steps. And to sum it all up, they have forgotten their maker (Hos 8:14). So far from knowing Him, they are living in total disregard of Him. Yet they still claim that He is their God. They don't know that they don't know Him.

How prone we are, especially when living in a nation of power and prosperity, to make power and prosperity the root of our hope and the desire of our hearts. Then we may say we are devoted to God, while setting our hearts on worshiping and serving our material blessings. How easily we may forget the God who is the true source of all security and blessing!

This message of Hosea is repeated in many other places throughout the Bible. In Jeremiah 3:4–5, after having pronounced judgment on Judah's idolatry, God says, "Have you not just now called to me, 'My father, you are the friend of my youth—will he be angry forever, will he be indignant to the end?' Behold, you have spoken, but you have done all the evil that you could." What an astonishing contradiction this is, between our words and our actions! If we really know God as father and friend, can we persist is doing our fill of evil? Shall we not instead seek to serve Him and walk in His ways throughout our whole life?

Also, Paul gives this same warning that "the day of the Lord will come like a thief in the night. While people are saying 'There is peace and security,' then sudden destruction will come upon them …" (1 Thes 5:3). It is all too easy to convince ourselves that all is well in our relationship with God, even while living in rejection of His revealed will.

Paul continues to speak to God's people: "But you are not in darkness, brothers, for that day to surprise you like a thief. For you are all children of light, children of the day … Since we belong to the day, let us be sober, having put on the breastplate of faith and love, and for a helmet the hope of salvation. For God has not destined us for wrath, but to obtain salvation through our Lord Jesus Christ, who died for us so that whether we are awake or asleep we might live with him" (1 Thes 5:4–10). What glorious, life-changing grace is given to us in Christ! Christ died for us so that we might live with Him! He has made us children of the light that we might walk in His light. By His eternal love He has destined us for salvation, so our lives are equipped with faith, love, and the hope of salvation.

Christ Himself is our highest good! He has redeemed us from sin and condemnation so that we might live with Him always. By faith in Christ we know the living God and will live with Him always as children of light. Let us be diligent to walk in the light of His love and show forth His glorious grace in our lives.

Reaping the Whirlwind
Hosea 8:7–14

A GREAT HYMN by Horatius Bonar begins with these words:
"Not what my hands have done, can save my guilty soul.
Not what my toiling flesh has borne can make my spirit whole."

Not only is it impossible for the works of our hands to save us, but if we rely on our own effort to make us right with God, then our accomplishments become the focus of our spiritual life. Then our works become a false hope, actually taking us away from the true and living God.

This is the lesson that Hosea 8:7 states in these words: "For they sow the wind, and they shall reap the whirlwind." He addresses a people who are busy and active and exerting great effort for the prosperity of their nation. They may well be laboring for worthwhile goals, but what are they working for? Is all their effort bringing them closer to God? They might believe that they are fulfilling God's purpose in a manner pleasing to Him, but Hosea says all their effort is like sowing seeds of wind. All their activity amounts to emptiness. There is nothing substantial, nothing to show, and nothing that lasts. We might suppose that the harvest from such seeds would be simply nothing, but actually it is worse than nothing. A tiny seed can produce a large crop and here the seed of wind turns into a harvest of whirlwind. The harvest for all their achieving is insubstantial and terribly destructive. The works of their hands have led only to disaster.

The rest of Hosea 8:7 speaks of the futility and uselessness of all their efforts. The grain produces no head, no fruitfulness. Their purpose in planting is completely unfulfilled. Even if it did produce grain for food, someone else would invade and steal it, leaving nothing to sustain life. Their labor has produced no security, no well-being.

This would be a desperate situation in an agrarian society that depended on their crops for food. But often fruitfulness of the land (or lack thereof) is a picture of the spiritual life of the nation. The tangible and material life is used to portray a spiritual reality. The decline of the nation's material well-being was serious but points to an underlying spiritual decline that is far more devastating. Hosea has already presented much evidence of spiritual weakness: no love, no covenant faithfulness, no justice, no integrity, no knowledge of God. Now he adds, no prosperity but only futility.

That the coming whirlwind is due to a spiritual emptiness is stated clearly in Hosea 8:14. Israel has built palaces and Judah has multiplied fortified cities. They have labored diligently to enjoy and preserve their material prosperity. But the whirlwind is coming, a judgment that will devour their cities and strongholds. None of it will last; their accomplishments will be reduced to nothing. What is the reason? Israel has forgotten its maker! The works of the people's hands have not brought them closer to God but taken them away from Him. Their delight in material blessings has removed their focus away from the giver of all blessings.

Chapter 8 of Hosea contains several other examples of works consumed by whirlwind. They not only made their own kings but also their own gods (Hos 8:4). Hosea declares that the work of a craftsman cannot possibly be a god (Hos 8:6). So far from bringing security, it will itself be smashed to pieces. Also, they have sought to make alliances with other nations for security (Hos 8:8–10). Hosea says they are behaving like a wandering wild donkey— stubborn, lost, and rebellious. Their alliances are like hiring a prostitute, forgetting their true lover and spending themselves to obtain illegitimate love. Soon they will be overwhelmed by the tribute owed to powerful nations around them. Even in their religious observance (Hos 8:11–13), reliance on their own effort brings only futility. They built many altars for sin offerings, but these become only many occasions for sinning. This is because the many laws revealing God's will were regarded as something distant and incomprehensible. When we profess to know God but live in opposition to His will and disregard His word, such hypocritical worship is not pleasing or acceptable to Him.

It is not as if Hosea is teaching that diligent labor is wrong, or that delight in prosperity is evil. But this is spoken in the context of transgressing God's covenant, rebelling against His laws, and rejecting His good purpose for them (Hos 8:2–3). When our hearts are far away from true devotion to God, all our effort becomes self-serving, seeking our own glory. Such diligence becomes idolatry. If our work becomes our god, then it will not bring us near to the one true God. Rather, it incurs His judgment.

We are a busy people, always working, always doing, consumed with activity. How can we avoid being overwhelmed and enslaved by our work? Can we find significance and satisfaction in our work? Can our work done in sincerity of heart be pleasing to the Lord?

Our works will only endure when they are built on the true foundation, which is Jesus Christ. In 1 Corinthians 3:10–11, Paul speaks of his own ministry as a wise master builder. The foundation he laid for the church at Corinth was the only sure foundation, our Lord Jesus Christ. Christ is the rock of our salvation; only He can bring us safely into God's presence. Only He can assure us of eternal blessings in His kingdom of glory. In Christ alone are our labors blessed so that we may be empowered to serve God acceptably in this world. If we build our lives on our own desires, our material gains, our own achievements, or our own glory, such work will not prosper or endure. All our works in life will only last for eternity when they flow out of hearts filled with joy and thanksgiving to Christ. Then we may steadfastly abound in the work of the Lord, assured that in Him our labor is not in vain (1 Cor 15:58).

Moses dares to pray in Psalm 90:17 that God would establish the works of our hands! This is the final request of an urgent prayer for gracious blessings in a time of great distress. Beginning in Psalm 90:12, he prays for a heart of wisdom to understand our life situation. Then he prays that we would be satisfied with knowing God's steadfast love and rejoice in it. He prays for future blessings of gladness instead of affliction, and prays that our children would know His works of glorious power. Finally he prays that the favor of our God would rest upon us. This is a prayer of one who is convinced that God is overwhelmingly gracious to His people and that we must live in utter dependence on that grace. God will establish the works of our hands in order to show forth His grace and power at work even in our little lives. Our accomplishments can only endure and prosper when done in reliance on Him and for His glory. How vital that we labor for what will endure forever!

When Rejoicing Fails

Hosea 9:1–9

IN OUR DAY and age, we find abundant food in our supermarkets. We tend to take for granted that our needs will be supplied without limit or termination. In cultures where people are dependent on growing their own food to survive, an abundant harvest is occasion for great rejoicing.

Chapter 9 of Hosea appears to be set in a harvest celebration, for Hosea 9:2 speaks of threshing floors and wine vats. Yet Hosea begins with surprising words: "Rejoice not, O Israel! Exult not like the peoples" (Hos 9:1). Hosea is raining on the parade of their harvest festival! Very likely this message was not well received by his neighbors. But Hosea hastens to justify this bearing of bad news. The people called by God's name have forsaken their God. Their prosperity is about to end and their rejoicing will cease.

Hosea is continuing his central theme of Israel's covenant-breaking, represented as marital unfaithfulness. In chapters 6–8, he has cited evidence of their loss of covenant blessings: no love, no faithfulness, no justice, no integrity, no knowledge of God, and no prosperity. Now he adds to the list: no joy, only punishment. Such are the consequences of living in disregard of God's gracious provision and rule.

Hosea 9:1 pictures Israel as a prostitute, forsaking her true lover and loving the wages of a false god. Previously, Hosea 2:5, and 2:8 had spoken of Israel's belief that its abundant harvest came from Baal and not from the Lord. Hosea 2:13 states that they celebrated their harvest feasts to Baal and went after other lovers but forgot the Lord. They believed their participation in the immoral worship of the pagan fertility cults would be rewarded by abundant crops. Hosea's name for this is forsaking the Lord and loving a prostitute's wages.

Hosea warns that if our joy relies on a false hope it cannot long endure. Such rejoicing is bound to fail. The true and living God is well able to reveal Baal's impotence by removing Israel's bountiful harvest (Hos 9:2). God will bring judgment upon all our false gods and show that we must depend on Israel's God for even our most basic needs.

Far worse is the declaration of coming exile. "They shall not remain in the land of the Lord" (Hos 9:3). The land belongs to the Lord; it was given as a blessing from Him. The people's removal of their trust in Him will result in removal from the land. The return to Egypt is a picture of return to bondage. In Assyria they will eat "unclean food" (Hos 9:3). Their food will not be a celebration of trust and thankfulness to the Lord but only whatever they can find to survive. Removal from the land represents removal from the presence of the Lord and His worship. As they have ceased to trust in the Lord, so their rejoicing will come to a drastic end.

In exile, any possibility of worship or fellowship with the Lord will be removed (Hos 9:4–6). Even their attempts to offer sacrifice will be displeasing to Him (Hos 9:4). It will be only an occasion for mourning, not rejoicing. Worship offered from cold hearts and evil hands will bring only defilement. Their sacrifice will be no more than an ordinary meal and fail to bring the people into the presence of the Lord. How can they observe the Lord's appointed festival in a foreign land (Hos 9:5)? They are removed from the Lord's land, leaving behind the destruction of their homeland, to die in a foreign country (Hos 9:6). All that was precious and comforting to them will be overcome with thorns. If our joy is not rooted in the gracious blessings of the Lord, that joy will not last. Hearts not overflowing with thankfulness to God for His abundant blessings will be overcome with sorrow.

For "the days of punishment have come" (Hos 9:7) and Israel's joy has ended. God will remember their iniquity and punish their sins (Hos 9:9). Their corruption is of a similar evil as the unspeakable sexual violence of Gibeah (Judges 19:22ff).

The hideous sin of despising God's law at Gibeah is repeated by their hatred of God's prophet! Hosea undoubtedly has incurred the wrath of his neighbors and knows the threat of physical violence. They now regard the prophet as a fool and madman. He is appointed by God to watch over the spiritual integrity of the nation. As God's spokesman he is to warn against any perversion in the life and worship of God's people. Yet he is continually confronted with dangerous snares and hatred, even in the midst of God's household. Here is appalling evidence of the depths to which Israel had sunk in forsaking their God and despising His word. Yet Hosea is faithful to his calling in announcing the terrible consequences when a people called by God's grace turns their back on Him to follow their own corrupt desires.

Israel's rejoicing failed as they ceased to trust and worship in the covenant faithfulness of their God. And yet we find unceasingly great joy is promised in the scriptures to those who bow before God's sovereign grace and seek to walk according to His revealed will. The psalmist says: "You have put more joy in my heart than they have when their grain and new wine abound" (Ps 4:7). Our joy is a blessing by God's grace. It doesn't depend on abundant material blessings. Joy comes from the presence of the Lord with us and our trust that He is working out His gracious purposes in our lives. Previously the psalmist had said in Psalm 4:3: "But know that the Lord has set apart the godly for himself; the Lord hears when I call to him." And "There are many who say, 'Who will show us some good? Lift up the light of your face upon us, O Lord!'" (Ps 4:6). True joy can only come from living in the grace and fellowship of the Lord our Redeemer.

On the night before he was crucified, Jesus spoke about His joy and ours! "I have told you this so that my joy may be in you and that your joy may be complete" (Jn 15:11). In John 16:22: "I will see you again and you will rejoice, and no one will take away your joy." And in John 17:13: "I say these things while I am still in the world, so that they may have the full measure of my joy within them." Jesus bequeaths His joy to His followers, a complete joy, joy that will endure. Clearly this is not joy that depends on circumstances but a joy grounded on the promises of God fulfilled in the finished ministry of Christ. Can we really believe that the greatest joys we will ever know are found in the grace of God revealed to sinners and in abiding in the love of Christ? Let us take Jesus at His word and find in Him our spiritual life filled with all His grace and joy.

They Shall Bear No Fruit

Hosea 9:10–17

THESE VERSES CONTAIN an utterly appalling and horrible warning of impending judgment. Israel will cease to bear fruit (Hos 9:16), and the termination of their fruitfulness centers on their children! First comes the dreadful promise (Hos 9:11) of "no birth, no pregnancy, no conception." This is followed by three appalling prophecies: "Even if they bring up children, I will bereave them till none is left" (Hos 9:12). "… but Ephraim must lead his children out to slaughter" (Hos 9:13). "Even though they give birth, I will put their beloved children to death" (Hos 9:16). Our hearts must recoil in horror at such dreadful words.

Ephraim was the largest and most powerful tribe of Israel, yet God will leave them no future as a distinct people. God will remove every blessing from His wayward unfaithful people, including even their descendants. These statements reflect the brutality of warfare in the ancient world, where invading forces usually showed no mercy upon the weak and vulnerable.

Hosea appears to be shocked at the horror of the message he is conveying. In Hosea 9:14 he says, "Give them O Lord—what will you give?" He scarcely knows how to pray after speaking such dreadful words about his own people. He concludes the verse by saying that it would be better if no children were born to the nation at all!

We, too, must wonder greatly at these terrible words. God not only is threatening judgment to come but also that He Himself will bring it to pass. How can our God, who is righteous, good, just, and loving, bring such awful desolation upon children? How can He bring this upon His covenant people who are called by His name?

We must always begin where the Bible begins when considering the condition of this sinful world, in all its misery and shame. When God created the heavens and earth, He immediately proclaimed them to be "very good" (Gen 1:31). This present world is not the world as God created it; humankind's sin has grievously corrupted it. The entire history of humanity has been filled with injustice, violence, cruelty, and suffering; it is the weakest who are always the most vulnerable. The world is not as bad as it possibly could be, as God has given restraints on human wickedness. Yet He has ordained that the misery and suffering of this present world will show forth the consequences of humanity's sinful rebellion and rejection of our creator. God declares in the second commandment (Ex 20:5) that He will visit the iniquity of the fathers on the children to the third and fourth generation of those who hate Him. Sinful patterns and idolatrous worship become established habits in human society and are passed on to future generations. Thus the descendants inherit God's condemnation for their father's rebellion.

This is all the more tragic because God speaks of His previous delight in His people Israel. These were the people He set apart for

His very own precious treasure. They were like delicious pleasing fruit (Hos 9:10). They were like a young palm tree (Hos 9:13), full of life and vitality. There was every expectation of future fruitfulness and usefulness. But now (Hos 9:16), all worthwhile produce is lost: "Ephraim is stricken; their root is dried up; they shall bear no fruit."

What went wrong? What provoked this threat of severe judgment on the people of Israel, where once there had been such promise of good fruit? The answer is also contained in Hosea 9:10: "But they came to Baal-peor and consecrated themselves to the thing of shame, and became detestable like the thing they loved." This event, recorded in Numbers 25, appears to be Israel's first departure into Baal worship. Even before entering the land of Canaan they had turned aside to Canaan's gods. They set their love upon a detestable thing. God says that in worshiping a detestable thing they also became detestable.

How devastating is the destructive power of idolatry in our spiritual life! As Israel had turned away from their Redeemer God who brought them out of bondage in Egypt, so now God would remove every blessing He had bestowed upon them. Their glory will fly away (Hos 9:11) and their true God will depart from them (Hos 9:12) and reject them (Hos 9:17). The depth of the broken relationship with their God is blatantly stated in Hosea 9:15. Because of their wicked rebellion, God began to hate them! He will disown them and love them no more. Their exile among the nations (Hos 9:17) is the result of failure to listen to God's voice and instruction.

God, our Creator and Redeemer, has every right to demand the unswerving allegiance of worship, love, and obedience. Our love for the false gods of worldliness and pride is a shameful hindrance. Such idols seek to remove the living God from His rightful place in the throne room of our hearts.

Yet glorious consolation may be found in Hosea's message, because this is not God's final word to Israel! God's purpose, through His prophet, is a call to repentance and a promise of extraordinary love and restoration for those who heed that call and seek the Lord their God with all their hearts. We may look ahead in wonder to the end of the story in Hosea 14, where we find words of overwhelming comfort and grace. "Return, O Israel, to the Lord your God" (Hos 14:1). "Say to Him, 'Take away all our iniquity'" (14:2). "In you the orphan finds mercy" (Hos 14:3). "I will heal their apostasy; I will love them freely" (Hos 14:4). And then comes the promise of astonishing fruitfulness (Hos 14:5–8): "I will be like the dew to Israel; he shall blossom like the lily; he shall take root like the trees of Lebanon; his shoots shall spread out; his beauty shall be like the olive, and his fragrance like Lebanon. They shall return and dwell beneath my shadow; they shall flourish like the grain; they shall blossom like the vine; their fame shall be like the wine of Lebanon. O Ephraim, what have I to do with idols? It is I who answer and look after you. I am like an evergreen cypress; from me comes your fruit."

The promise of this glorious spiritual fruitfulness points us to the fullness of our redemption in Jesus Christ. Consider the words of Jesus (Jn 15:7–11): "If you abide in me, and my words abide in you, ask whatever you wish, and it will be done for you. By this my Father is glorified, that you bear much fruit and so prove to be my disciples. As the Father has loved me, so have I loved you. Abide in my love. If you keep my commandments, you will abide in my love, just as I have kept my father's commandments and abide in his love. These things I have spoken to you, that my joy may be in you, and that your joy may be full."

Hosea is showing us the pathway to true spiritual fruit, the fullness of vital union with the living God. This is the Father's design and desire for His vineyard. Such everlasting fruit can only

Ephraim Shall Be Put to Shame
Hosea 10:1–10

CHAPTER 10 CONCLUDES Hosea's warnings of judgment that will surely come if the people of Israel persist in their covenant unfaithfulness to the Lord. Chapters 6–9 have described at great length that unfaithfulness and its terrible consequences: no love, no covenant-keeping, no justice, no integrity, no knowledge of God, no prosperity, no joy, no fruitfulness. Now Hosea adds a prophecy of despair and a promise of no hope and no future. The Lord's case for divorce from His unfaithful bride is complete; nothing is left but guilt and shame. Ephraim shall be put to shame (Hos 10:6), and shall be ashamed of his idol. God will bring to a complete end both Israel's false gods and their wicked kings.

The reign of King Jeroboam in Samaria had been a time of great strength, deliverance, and prosperity (2 Kings 14). Israel was like a luxuriant vine (Hosea 10:1), full of fruit, improving his country. But Jeroboam had also led the people in continual idolatrous worship. As their prosperity increased, so also did their altars and pillars to their false gods. Moses had warned the people about this sin (Dt 8:14). He predicted that when the Lord had brought them into a good land and provided them with wealth and prosperity, then their hearts would be lifted up and they would forget the Lord who was the source of all these blessings. And so it had happened, for now they were giving to the pagan gods of Canaan the credit for the good gifts they had received from the hand of the Lord! Hosea says their hearts were false and deceitful (Hos 10:2), impure in devotion to the God who they professed, divided between serving two masters. He promises that their guilt will weigh heavily upon them and the Lord will bring to an end all their false worship. Their duplicity of heart could only lead the nation to weakness, loss, and shame.

After the reign of Jeroboam, the kingdom quickly deteriorated into weakness and chaos. Hosea 10:3 observes that their present kings had seized power by deceit and violence, not through their reverence for God. The resulting rulers were so weak and ineffective that there might as well have been no king at all! Yet how could even a powerful king be of help when they had turned away from the Lord? The Lord Himself was to be their true king, but they said, "We have no king, for we do not fear the Lord" (Hos 10:3). The resulting decline of justice had become painfully evident (Hos 10:4). The words of their kings were deceitful, their oaths meaningless, their promises unreliable. Their administration of justice now resembled poisonous weeds springing up where useful crops should have grown, doing more harm than good. Hosea predicts a time soon to come (Hos 10:7) when Samaria's kings will perish completely. They shall float away like a twig on the water, utterly impotent and useless. So far from being a source of strength and glory, their king will bring only defeat and shame.

The weakness of these kings grew out of their heart's devotion to the false gods they followed. God now promises to condemn these pagan idols as utterly useless, and to bring them to shame.

The calf idol at Beth-aven, which had been their glory and rejoicing (Hos 10:5), will bring only trembling and mourning. (Beth-aven means "house of evil." It is used here to designate the sins of Bethel, which means "house of God.") For a second time, the glory will have departed from Israel (see 1 Sam 4:21). It will be carried off to Assyria as tribute to the king, and its places of worship destroyed (Hos 10:8). This would be the ultimate defeat and insult to a people when the idol they worshiped as their source of strength is carried off as plunder in subjection to a foreign king. The false god they had trusted for their security and prosperity would be shown to be completely impotent and helpless. The nation, together with the idol they worshiped, shall be ashamed (Hos 10:6) and humiliated.

For God will show Himself to be the almighty king and sovereign Lord. He will be pleased to discipline His people (Hos 10:10) and pour out judgment on false worship. He will purify them as those sanctified to Himself, by destroying all that is in sinful rebellion against Him. He will gather other nations against Israel and remove His wall of protection from around them. In the coming war, Israel's people shall be bound up as captives because of their double iniquity (Hos 10:10). This appears to be a reference to two places where their sinful rebellion was especially heinous. God regarded their idol worship at Bethel (Hos 10:5) to be as hideous as the crimes and violence at Gibeah (Hosea 10:9, again referring to the unspeakable evil recorded in Judges 19). War and destruction resulted from the crimes of Gibeah and now again war against their unjust deeds will overtake them. As Israel has continued in shameful wickedness, so war will sweep away their shameful kings along with the detestable gods they worshiped.

A legacy of weakness, shame, and destruction will result in despair and utter terror (Hos 10:8): "They shall say to the mountains, 'Cover us,' and to the hills, 'Fall on us.'" Hosea predicts the words of those overtaken by total loss and desolation because of their sinful rebellion. Better to be buried alive than to be subjected to the devastating wrath of a holy God! This verse is used twice in the New Testament when predictions are spoken regarding overwhelming judgments to come. Jesus, in Luke 23:30, spoke concerning the coming destruction of Jerusalem as a consequence of rejecting their Messiah. But John, in Revelation 6:16, expands this to warn of the final judgment coming on the whole of humanity who are opposed to Christ and persecuting His church. The judgments of this present age are a small foretaste of the great day of the wrath of the lamb. Jesus surely is the Lamb of God who humbled himself and in unfathomable love was submissive even to a shameful death on a cross. He took on Himself the awful wrath of God for the sins of all who call upon Him for salvation, to purchase their redemption. But He will be revealed on that day as the judge who pours out His righteous wrath on those who persist in sinful rebellion against His righteous rule and gracious gift of salvation.

Paul speaks of our glorious hope of deliverance from this judgment in 1 Thessalonians 1:9–10: "… you turned to God from idols to serve the living and true God, and to wait for his Son from heaven, whom he raised from the dead, Jesus who delivers us from the wrath to come." What Hosea spoke to ancient Israel stands as a warning to people in all ages. There is a coming wrath upon all the unrighteousness of those who suppress the truth of the gospel of Christ. Jesus delivers us from the judgment of God! He rose from death to deliver us from the power of sin and will return in glory to deliver us from the presence of sin. Humanity in every age must turn away from the idols of power, wealth, lust, and pride to worship and serve the living God with our whole heart and soul. Jesus, the Lord of glory, risen from the dead, now gives eternal life to all who look to Him in faith. Jesus, the righteous judge of all humankind, is also the only one able to deliver us from this coming wrath. Let us flee to Jesus for refuge (Heb 6:18), that we may find a sure and steadfast anchor for our soul. For whoever believes in Him will not be put to shame (Rom 9:33). "God is not ashamed to be called their God, for He has prepared for them a city" (Heb 11:16). Let us not be ashamed of the gospel (Rom 1:16) but glory in the cross, the power of God for all who are being saved (1 Cor 1:18).

Break Up Your Fallow Ground
Hosea 10:11–15

HOSEA 10:12 IS an amazingly gracious call to repentance. "Break up the fallow ground, for it is time to seek the Lord, that He may come and rain righteousness upon you." These words can only be described as amazing and gracious when considered in light of the terrible indictment of sin and promise of impending judgment contained in the preceding chapters. Chapters 4–10 are a devastating portrayal of Israel's hardness of heart, the people's lack of righteousness, and their failure to seek the Lord their God. Yet God's wondrous love persists in seeking reconciliation with His wayward people.

Previously, in chapters 4 and 5, God took the part of an offended husband suing for divorce from Israel, His unfaithful wife. There followed (in Hos 6:1–3) a most kind and merciful call to Israel to repent of their spiritual adultery and return to Him. Since that call was disregarded, there is set forth in chapters 6–10 the grounds for divorce. His church, His bride, had transgressed His covenant and the people's desertion of their God had brought forth abundant crimes and injustice. Israel, the congregation of people called to be consecrated to the Lord, had lost all love, joy, integrity, fruitfulness, and hope. Yet even in the midst of threats of dreadful destruction of their kingdom, God still pleads with His people to escape the coming wrath by returning to Him with all their hearts. How amazing is God's patience and compassion toward sinful men and women! Over and over again He entreats sinful people to abandon their hardhearted rebellion and seek the blessings of His covenant love. Now in Christ He has delivered us from our sinful revolt, and in great mercy has brought us into all the blessings of His eternal kingdom. How little do we deserve any thought of kindness from Him. Yet how lovingly He turns our hearts to Christ, renewing our souls to seek forgiveness and restoration!

Hosea tells a story of God's kindness and severity. "Ephraim was a trained calf that loved to thresh, and I spared her fair neck" (Hos 10:11). God regarded His people with kindness and delight. While training them in godliness He also spared them from hard labor (threshing was much easier than plowing). And His people loved to thresh. They had delighted in the privilege of service to the Lord! Their yoke of obedience had been easy and their burden light. But now they had chosen the difficult way. Because of their covenant rebellion, God will subject them to a heavy yoke and hard labor. Now they harrow only for themselves and their joyful service of their God has been neglected. Hosea 10:13 explains how grievously their labor became distorted. They plowed and planted iniquity, producing a harvest of abundant injustice, and so they ate the rotten fruit of lies. Their trust was now in their own wisdom, their own ways, and in worldly power. The call to repentance is urgent and vital. God's impending judgment on them is very severe.

Yet Hosea points the way to a far more superior harvest. This abundant harvest of God's steadfast love is brought forth in our lives by God's gift of righteousness, shed upon His people like a gentle rain from heaven. God, who is rich in mercy, extends the grace of repentance and the hope of renewal! "Break up the fallow ground" (Hos 10:12)—the hard and stony ground of our hearts, a land neglected, fruitless and useless. Bring on the plowing with the word of God by the powerful working of His Holy Spirit. Break up the hard soil of sinful patterns of life, long established and unyielding. Soften the ground with divine love and regeneration, that we may be given new hearts of flesh instead of hearts of stone. Then we can plant seeds of a righteous desire for doing God's will and bring forth in our lives a golden harvest of steadfast love. Hosea proclaims, "… it is time to seek the Lord" (Hos 10:12) in worship, giving glory to Him alone as God. In true worship we turn our hearts away from every false god and every ungodly desire and call upon Him as our only strength and hope. For He promises to those who diligently seek Him that He will surely come with a rain of righteousness that will bring forth in our lives a gift of glorious fruit for Him.

God's call to repentance is gracious and genuine. It is also of the utmost urgency, for His warning of coming destruction is dire and very real (Hos 10:14–15). War and destruction are on the horizon and Israel's military strength will not prevail. Their people, even women and children, will be subjected to the most barbaric cruelty. These atrocities had already been manifested by Shalman (Shalmaneser, the king of Assyria in 2 Kings 17:3) at Beth-Arbel (location unknown but probably a town in northern Israel). Hosea proclaims the same horrors that shall come to Bethel, where the seed of idolatrous worship produced a harvest of gross injustice and great evil. Their king and kingdom will be overthrown suddenly, as if overnight, so that when morning comes he will have utterly disappeared. How essential and urgent to break up the hard ground of sinful rebellion and to seek the Lord's favor with humble and contrite hearts!

The apostle Paul speaks of this same spiritual sowing and reaping in Galations 6:7–9: "Do not be deceived: God is not mocked, for whatever one sows, that will he also reap. For the one who sows to his own flesh will from the flesh reap corruption, but the one who sows to the Spirit will from the Spirit reap eternal life. And let us not grow weary of doing good, for in due season we will reap, if we do not give up." This contrast of flesh and spirit is highlighted in Galations 5:16–17, where the two are in strong opposition, their desires contrary and in continual warfare with each other. The flesh is our sinful nature that is intent on following desires and priorities opposed to God's rule. The Spirit of Christ dwells in all who call upon Him as Savior and Lord. He is the Spirit of holiness who works true righteousness in their lives. Paul highlights the immense contrast between these two harvests, the deeds of the flesh and the fruit of the Spirit (Gal 5:19–23). Christ breaks up the fallow ground of our hard, sinful, and useless hearts, making us fertile soil to bring forth righteous fruit. He is the power of God who renews and revives our inmost being, so that we desire and strive for all that is holy and pleasing to Him.

Let us sow wisely, investing time, energy, and effort in the lasting harvest of righteousness, love, and faithfulness. Feeding the desires of the sinful nature will produce in us only further corruption and futility. Following the leading of God's Spirit, seeking to do His will revealed in His word, we will reap an eternal harvest of spiritual riches.

Israel, the Prodigal Son

Hosea 11:1–4

HOSEA IS THE prophet of love. His primary purpose is to show forth the love of God for His covenant people and call them to live in the glorious light of that love. He uses the strongest pictures of love that we know, those of family relationships. For ten chapters he has used the illustration of marriage. Israel is the precious bride betrothed to the Lord but who has turned away to seek other lovers. Yet He diligently pursues her and seeks to restore their broken relationship. In the next three chapters the image changes. The Lord declares, "When Israel was a child, I loved him, and out of Egypt I called my son" (Hos 11:1). Now the picture is of a Father's undying love for His rebellious son.

For Israel is a son gone astray. Chapters 11–13 contain six recollections of Israel's past glory, when God's kindness and care provided for their needs and made them a strong nation. But each of these events is immediately followed by Israel's turning away from the love of their Father. They worship other gods on which they rely for their material prosperity. They fail to respond with love for Him or acknowledge that the good gifts they received have come from God's hand. Yet God's love continues with great patience. While He will chastise them for their rebellion, His love for them never falters. He desires their return to His fatherly compassion and He even promises that His loving discipline will restore to them all the richest of blessings.

God reminds the people of Israel that His love was placed upon them from their very beginning. This love was made manifest in the calling of Israel out of slavery in Egypt. God's love rescues and delivers. It is a love that brings His people into great peace and well-being. It is a love that chooses, for no other people ever were delivered out of bondage as Israel was. It is love that longs to possess, that claimed Israel as His very own. It is a love that redeemed an enslaved people and adopted them as His children. It is an amazing, astonishing love that revealed to the world all His mercy and compassion for fallen humanity. By that supreme love He would powerfully deliver His people out of bondage to evil, destroying the tyranny and oppression of false gods.

Israel's tragic disdain for God's wondrous love is summarized in Hosea 11:2: "The more they were called, the more they went away." Israel becomes the prodigal son! The love of the Father is rejected; instead of following His call they turn away. Hosea 11:12 continues: "They kept sacrificing to the Baals and burning offerings to idols." They who knew the great deliverance by the hand of the Lord were now depending on other gods to find help and prosperity.

How vital is true worship in our life of service to God! As He has called us to be His adopted children, so He alone must be the center of all our loyalty and affection. The foundation of our spiritual life is the grateful acknowledgment of his abundant blessings. We must daily call upon Him as our only hope and help for all we need. We cannot long continue to walk in communion with our God apart from abiding in devoted worship.

Yet the Father's astonishing love had brought the richest blessings to His children (Hos 11:3–4)! God speaks here of His active love. Six times He says, "It was I" who provided for their most basic needs. The picture is of the gentle striving and caring of a human father for his young children. Is this not also a poignant description of God's providing for the growth and nurture of all the children He adopts to Himself in Jesus Christ? We are all like spiritual babies, helpless and utterly dependent upon the strength and kindness of our heavenly Father.

How does our Father love us? Let us count the ways. First, He trains us to walk in His ways, following His goodness and kindness, as children imitating their father. Second, He holds us up by our arms to keep us from falling away from Him. In those times when we feel too weak to continue in our journey with Him, He upholds us by His powerful hands. Then He heals us, even when we are not aware of His presence. From the brokenness and sickness of our soul He delivers us and restores us to wholeness. He also leads us with cords of kindness and bands of love. These are real cords of grace that bind us to Himself. He does not leave us to wander in dark and dangerous places of sin and foolishness, but He guides us in paths of righteousness for our own good. His every impulse guides our steps into what is true and good and beautiful. His everlasting love will safely lead us to all the riches of His grace in eternal glory. He is like one who eases our yoke, even taking upon Himself our terrible burden of sin. The yoke He places on us is easy, so that we may serve Him with thankfulness and joy. Finally, He bends down to feed us. Not only does He provide our daily bread, but He nourishes our souls with the bread of life come down to us from heaven. How good and gracious is our heavenly Father, providing for all our needs and filling our lives with glorious blessings!

Hosea is giving us a wonderful prophecy of the love of God that would be revealed to the world in Jesus Christ. In Christ we are delivered from the dominion of sin, adopted as God's children, and abundantly provided with everything we need for life and godliness. By heavenly grace God has come down to us in our Lord Jesus Christ. We are given full assurance that by partaking of Him we may find true spiritual life and strength that only He can provide. So we entrust all of our heart and life to such a Father who gives good gifts to His children.

And Jesus also was called out of Egypt by the love and power of the Father (Mt 2:15). Matthew teaches us that Jesus's flight into Egypt was a fulfillment of the prophecy of Hosea 11:1. Jesus, like Israel, fled to Egypt as a temporary refuge from danger. Both Israel and Jesus were delivered from powerful enemies by God's almighty hand. Both are designated "my Son," revealing God's special love and care!

Israel's exodus out of Egypt is a prophecy of God's provision of redemption from sin for all His people in Christ. Though Jesus had no sin, He so identified with His sinful people that His exodus was on their behalf, leading them triumphantly out of the domain of sin and Satan and into the promised land of eternal glory. Jesus suffered all the hatred and oppression of this sinful world for us, so that His deliverance would be our deliverance. God preserved Jesus's life so that He could fulfill all the work as our mediator in reconciling us to God. As God delivered Israel out of Egypt, so He also called Christ to triumph over sin and misery for all His church. The fulfillment is that by Christ's life and ministry, God has called all His children out of slavery to sin.

For Christians, too, are prodigal sons and daughters. We have all gone astray from the home of our heavenly Father in sinful rebellion and ungodly living. And yet by the Father's great love we are enabled to return to Him with sorrow and repentance, trusting that we will find unspeakably great rest and comfort in His Fatherly care and love. And that love He has forever revealed by sending His beloved Son to die for His church to cleanse us from all sin and receive us into His eternal home.

I Am God and Not a Man
Hosea 11:5–11

WE MAY IMAGINE that God acts and reasons in ways similar to us, yet scripture often reminds us that God's ways are not our ways and His thoughts not like our thoughts (Is 55:8). So we should regularly expect to be astonished at God's dealings with humankind. He declares this in Hosea 11:9, with these words: "For I am God and not a man, the Holy One in your midst." How radically different He is from us and how far above our understanding! He is pure and undefiled, exalted and separate from sinners, a consuming fire able to destroy all that stands opposed to Him. Yet The Holy One, the creator and sustainer of the universe, is among us! Shouldn't that fill us with trembling and awe? He has come among us in great mercy as a refining fire (Mal 3:2), not to consume but to purify and transform our weak and lowly lives into something beautiful for Him.

In this passage Hosea shows the shocking and surprising wonder of God's workings among humanity. In three ways he shows how different God's ways are from our ways. First, God is distressed by human sin, while we so often are complacent about our sin. In Hosea 11:5–7, God is indignant over the sin of His people. "They have refused to return to me ... My people are bent on turning away from me." God takes such rebellion seriously: "Assyria shall be their king ... the sword shall rage against their cities, consume the bars of their gates, and devour them ..." God powerfully uses trials and sorrows to turn us away from our sin, prompting us to seek the grace and mercy of our heavenly Father.

We become comfortable with our sinful habits, so we are contented to continue in them. This is the situation in Hosea 11:7, where Israel calls out to God, but He does not come to their aid. In the same verse He speaks of them as "My people" but says they are bent on turning away from Him. God in love had called them to Himself (Hos 11:2), but they have turned away and worshiped other gods and followed their own counsels (Hos 11:6). They did not recognize as very serious the sin of turning to other gods. He is no longer their God! Can we claim to be living in fellowship with our God while at the same time ignoring His counsel and direction for our lives? God is not complacent about our sin. We must not take our sin lightly, but grieve over it as God does.

But a second way in which God's ways are not our ways is in His unswerving faithfulness and enduring covenant love. Hosea 11:8–9, perhaps more vividly than anywhere else in scripture, sets forth God's passionate love for His people and His compassionate anguish over their sinful rebellion. Israel is His prodigal child (Hos 11:2). God is like a human father who must discipline His wayward child. His love for his child is not at all diminished, though he is deeply grieved by such willful disobedience. The father of the prodigal son (Lk 15:20) gives us a glorious picture of God's rich compassion and mercy in welcoming and embracing His wayward children when they repent.

But in another sense, God's mercy far surpasses anything in human experience. We might expect the righteous judge to pour out condemnation on those awful sins listed in Hosea 11:5-7. Instead, God's wondrous love is expressed in deep anguish and compassion that triumphs over the sins of His people. He cries out, "How can I give you up? How can I hand you over? My heart recoils within me" (Hos 11:8). God is dismayed at our sins, yet His mercy grows warm and tender. His heart recoils and is appalled at the thought of giving up on the people He loved and called to be His own treasured possession! The people of His covenant love He will not destroy in wrath, as He did Admah and Zeboiim, towns that were destroyed along with Sodom and Gomorrah (Dt 29:23), forever a reminder of the power of God's burning wrath. The Lord will not abandon the Fatherly love so wonderfully portrayed in Hosea 11:3–4 but will fulfill the purpose of His love in calling Israel to Himself (Hos 11:1). He will show Himself to be compassionate and kind to the weak and lowly. His faithfulness and patient redeeming love will move us to respond with heartfelt devotion and adoration. God's ways are not our ways. How hard for us to understand the strange workings of God's rich mercy to sinful people!

A third way in which God's ways are different from our ways is that His powerful grace is able to reconcile sinful people to Himself (Hos 11:10–11). We might seek vengeance and retaliation against someone who offends us. God, while He may chastise our wrongdoing, does so only to purify and set us apart as people consecrated to Himself. He seeks a renewed relationship of love and trust with his wayward children. He softens our rebellious hearts so that we may follow after the Lord (Hos 11:10) with fervent devotion.

God's claim on the souls of His people is like the roar of a lion, issuing forth with power and authority! It announces His fierce and terrible destruction of His enemies. But His roar is also a renewed call to the children of His love. It is a sovereign call of irresistible grace because His voice changes the direction of our hearts to seek and serve the Lord. When He roars they will answer His call, they will come with trembling. They will tremble in fear and weakness and humility at the awesome majesty and holiness of the Lord. But coming to Him, they will find unfathomable riches of His love and mercy. For He declares that He will return them to their homes (Hos 11:11). He will dwell with them there forever and they will enjoy the peace and security that only can be found in His love and friendship.

They shall come trembling not only from Assyria in the east, and Egypt to the south, but also from the west (Hos 11:10). The picture is that God will draw a people to Himself from every direction, from every part of the world. This was partially fulfilled when the Persian kings were moved by God to return Israel from their exile. But there will be a far greater gathering as God calls a vast number from the whole world into faith in the God of Israel and obedience to His Messiah. Here is a gracious prophecy that Christ would call to Himself children from every direction and location of the earth.

While many question how a loving God could bring such terrible wrath and destruction on people (Hos 11:5–7), perhaps a more difficult question is how a God of justice could pardon sinful people and receive them as His own children. God's ways are not our ways! Romans 3:26 declares that God is both "just and the justifier of the one who has faith in Jesus." God is just. He must condemn sin. He has put forward another, one who is perfect in righteousness, to endure the death penalty for the sins of His covenant people. God gave His own Son, Jesus Christ, as an atoning sacrifice, to cover over the guilt of our sin and turn aside the wrath of God. So God who is just also justifies sinners!

He manifests His righteousness in us by clothing us with Christ's righteousness and declaring us to be righteous in His sight. This righteousness comes to us as a gift of His grace and is received by faith alone. The incredible blessings of forgiveness and restoration that Hosea declared to Israel so long ago are also promised at the present time to all who receive by faith the free gift of salvation in Jesus Christ. God has indeed done more for us than we could ever think or imagine. He has reconciled sinners to Himself in incomprehensible grace.

The LORD is His Memorial Name

Hosea 11:12–12:6

IN CHAPTER 12, Hosea continues to develop the theme of Israel as the prodigal son. He draws a parallel between the life of the patriarch Jacob and the nation Israel descended from him. Both Jacob and his descendants received promises of rich blessing, both strayed from God, both struggled against God, and both were graciously called to return to God, to hear His voice and walk in union and fellowship with Him. God has wondrously used the spiritual struggles of Jacob and his descendants to show forth the riches of redemption in Christ.

Hosea appeals to Israel to remember! He declares, "The LORD is His memorial name" (Hos 12:5). He wants the people to remember their God, His covenant, His deeds, and His promises. Hosea identifies the only true God using His covenant name, the LORD (Jahweh), the name revealed to Moses long after Jacob was dead. His covenant faithfulness, made known to Jacob, is to be remembered forever by His people as their only hope for spiritual blessing. Hosea calls to mind their history: that both Jacob and his descendants were kept under the merciful rule of their covenant-keeping God. Jacob met with God at Bethel and "there God spoke with us" (Hos 12:4). Hosea, writing some twelve hundred years after Jacob, is sure that the words God spoke to Jacob were for "us"! God's covenant promises were not for Jacob alone but for all his descendants and for all those who would by faith call upon the God of Jacob to be their God and Savior. For at that time (Gen 35:11–12), God conferred on Jacob the promises made to his forefathers and also extended those promises to Jacob's descendants. God not only revealed His existence and His will to Jacob but also His redeeming love to Jacob's spiritual descendants, who would put their trust in this same God. Our only hope for finding communion with God is His faithfulness to remember His covenant promises for His people.

God had highlighted a radical change in Jacob's spiritual life and character by changing his name to Israel. Hosea 12:3 refers to both names. Jacob means "he grasps the heel" (alternatively, "he deceives"). Israel means "he strove with God and prevailed" (Gen 32:28). Jacob's early life displays an aptitude for using ungodly means to manipulate others in order to achieve his own desires. He struggled against God and even prevailed against the angel (Gen 32:22ff). But when confronted with overwhelming power, his confidence in his accomplishments was swept away. Seeing himself as lost and undone before a holy God, he pleaded with tears for God's blessing (Hos 12:4) and found favor from Him. God graciously extended to him the covenant blessings promised to Abraham and Isaac, to be His God, to make him into a great nation, and to be a blessing to all families on the earth. Hosea presents Jacob's life as a vivid portrayal of God's transforming power in the lives of His people.

However, Jacob's descendants were following the way of the prodigal. Israel's spiritual condition at the time of Hosea's writing is far different from the future glories promised in Hosea 11:10–11. Ephraim (the northern kingdom of Israel) persisted in lies and deceit, falsehood and violence (Hos 11:12–12:1). Thus, all their activity led only to futility: "feeding on the wind" (Hos 12:1). But, like the superheated east wind from the desert, their ungodly desires and pursuits would eventually consume them. They sought security from ungodly and unreliable foreign nations by forming alliances and profitable trade relations (oil carried to Egypt, Hos 12:1). Also, the southern kingdom of Judah "is unruly against God, even against the faithful Holy One" (Hos 11:12 NIV). (While the meaning of the Hebrew text for this verse is disputed, there is good evidence for the NIV translation.) Both kingdoms were liable to punishment from the Lord for their rebellious ways (Hos 11:2).

So here, too, God through Hosea was confronting Israel with their sin and rebellion. But once again He graciously and gently calls the people to repentance (Hos 11:6), as He had called their ancestor Jacob. This call, not by the angel of the Lord but by His prophet, came with the same intensity of divine grace as the soul-redeeming call to Jacob had come. He reminds them to remember the kindness of God who remembers His promises to His people.

Hosea 12:6 contains four wonderful words of blessing for all of God's children when we have strayed into sin and then come to our senses. First, repentance is by the help of our God. God leads our hearts and enables us to repent! We must believe that God's awesome power is available to those who desire to turn away from sin and follow in the way of life He has marked out. We may feel that the grip of sin on us is strong and unbreakable. We know our own weakness in our struggle against sin. Like Jacob in the agony of his dislocated hip, utterly emptied of any ability to prevail against God, we too must cry out to God in our weakness for His blessing.

Second, repentance means we are to return to our God. Like the prodigal we must say to Him "Father I have sinned against heaven and before you" (Lk 15:21). Jesus gives us great assurance that our heavenly Father will welcome us with compassion and joy. While our sin is a grievous offense against a loving Father, in repentance we again seek communion with a love that is immense beyond our imagining.

Third, we are to walk unswervingly in a path of love and justice. Repentance is a change in lifestyle that will radically alter our relationships with other people. If we are seeking to live in God's favor, we will strive to put off the old patterns of behavior and walk in a manner worthy of the Lord. No more may we live by oppression and deceit, striving for our own advantage at the expense of others. If we have the least understanding of the mercy and compassion of our God, we will feel compelled to imitate that mercy in our dealings with others.

Fourth, to wait continually for our God means to live in dependence on Him, seeking to live under the direction of His will, and habitually following in obedience to His leadership. "Waiting for God" implies confidence of future blessings. While the future is unknown to us, we may be assured that God holds the future in His hand and will graciously guide our steps into all His good will. Everyone whom God calls to Himself as children in His heavenly family must undergo the same radical transformation of life and character as Jacob did.

Today God still remembers His covenant promises spoken to Abraham, Isaac, and Jacob to be the God of a vast multitude of people from every nation on the earth. As He met with Jacob at Bethel to reveal His covenant blessings, so He continues to proclaim the same blessings of redemption in Christ throughout the world. Jacob's heavenly stairway (Gen 28:12) is fulfilled now in our Lord Jesus Christ, who promised, "You will see heaven opened, and the angels of God ascending and descending on the Son of Man" (Jn 1:51). Heavenly grace is sent down to humankind through our Lord Jesus. Upon Him we are raised up to heavenly glory. He is still calling His wayward children home to partake of the blessings of His fatherly love. How vital, then, that we perpetually remember the name by which we are called as members of His spiritual family. Shall not all our thoughts, the attitudes of our hearts, and the direction of our steps be subject to the dominion of Him who has opened heaven to us?

They Cannot Find in Me Iniquity or Sin

Hosea 12:7–14

HOSEA'S GREAT CALL to repentance (Hos 12:6) is God's amazing gracious solution to Israel's continual deceit, falsehood, and violence (Hos 11:12–12:1). Israel is urged to follow their forefather Jacob, who turned away from such sins and found forgiveness and favor with God. Their need for repentance is continued in Hosea 12:7, where the word "merchant" is really the word "Canaanite." Apparently the land of Canaan was known for merchants who grew rich by cheating and deception. Hosea says that Ephraim (the northern kingdom of Israel) had become just like the pagan Canaanites! Ephraim was seeking prosperity by means of false balances and oppression.

Ephraim's response is devastating (Hos 12:8): "I have found wealth for myself; in all my labors they cannot find in me iniquity or sin." This outright denial of the wrongs listed in the previous verse is distressing but not surprising because the people are in love with their sin. "They love to oppress" (Hos 12:7). They may claim to have been fortunate and that they worked hard to acquire great wealth. They might even claim that God had prospered their business. Of course, there is nothing wrong with being successful in business, as long as it is done by honesty and integrity in accord with God's law. In gaining wealth, as in all of life, we must follow in the two great commandments, to love God first in all of life and to love our neighbor as ourself. How empty our spiritual life must be if we can ignore these two central priorities of our existence and then insist that we have done no wrong.

Denial of our sinful condition is evidence of complete spiritual deadness. It displays a tragic lack of understanding of God's revealed truth. It shows that we are deceived about our own life, and worst of all, it makes God out to be a liar (1 Jn 1:8,10).

Hosea answers their foolish denial of sin using several arguments. His method is to again recall God's incredible mercy and faithfulness to Israel in past generations. First he reminds them of the absolute necessity of following God's commandments. "I am the LORD your God from the land of Egypt" (Hos 12:9) is a clear reference to the giving of the ten commandments. The only true God, the God of the covenant, gives Himself to the people of Israel as "your God." He has taken them as His chosen people, called them by His name, and graciously redeemed them out of bondage. Shall not this great God have the right to rule and direct the lives of this people? Are they not bound to receive and obey all He has commanded them? Isn't this the only proper response for such a powerful deliverance? How much more should we, who know the fulfillment of all God's promises of redemption in Christ, be diligent to walk in a manner worthy of our Lord with great joy and thankfulness?

Second, He points to their need for humility. "I will again make you dwell in tents" (Hos 12:9). The Feast of Tabernacles was a time of rejoicing because of God's great provision and blessing to His people, but also a reminder that He had made them live in booths when He brought them out of the land of Egypt (Lev 23:43). They had endured great hardship for forty years in the wilderness before entering into the riches of the promised land. This verse is a warning that their rebellion against God's commands would result in the coming exile, where they would again be removed from worldly comforts. God's rich blessings come as free gifts from His gracious hand, and are to be received with humble thankfulness. We are to walk humbly with our God (Micah 6:8), seeking to honor Him in all our ways.

A third response to their denial of sin is a reminder (Hos 12:10) that God had spoken to their fathers at many times and in various ways. God had revealed Himself directly to the people through His prophets. He had spoken as the sovereign King over heaven and earth and yet had declared His love for Israel, whom He chose to be a people consecrated to Himself. He had taught them to worship and serve Him and to live by every word from His mouth. How could they now ignore such a great gift of the knowledge of the Lord and all His ways? How imperative it is that we also should receive, believe, and obey the word of Jesus Christ, God's greatest and final prophet.

Fourth, He warns them of the futility of their sinful ways. "If there is iniquity … they will surely come to nothing" (Hos 12:11). Hosea has already condemned the sins of Gilead ("a city of evildoers, tracked with blood" [Hos 6:8]) and Gilgal ("every evil of theirs is in Gilgal" [Hos 9:15]). He says their sacrifices are useless; their altars are merely heaps of stones taking up space in a field. These cities, which had a glorious history of service to God, were now hopelessly lost and wayward.

Hosea 12:12–13 gives a vivid contrast between Jacob the sinful man and Israel the people under God's grace. Jacob fled in fear, but God brought Israel back by great power. Jacob fled alone, but God sent a prophet to lead Israel. Jacob served (slaved) for a wife, but the Lord brought Israel out of slavery into the promised land. Jacob guarded sheep, but God's prophet guarded Israel. Jacob worked to gain his wife, but God chose Israel by free grace to be His bride! What a powerful reminder of the futility of seeking to serve God by our own effort and ingenuity! How rich is God's provision of grace and kindness for His people! Having begun in the majestic power and grace of God, should we not continue in thankful dependence on that glorious grace every moment of every day?

Hosea 12:14 gives the final and definitive verdict concerning all denial of sin. We are guilty of disgraceful deeds that bitterly provoke God's justice. If we persist in unrepentant rejection of His gift of grace, we will bear the severe judgment for our wrongdoing.

Ephraim's boast of sinless prosperity (Hosea 12:8) proved to be empty and false. Could we ever find someone without iniquity or sin? If found, wouldn't we desire to follow and learn from that person? Surely such a person would bring great benefit to humanity. Those who knew Jesus best gave precisely this testimony of His life. "He committed no sin" (1 Pet 2:22). "In Him there is no sin" (1 Jn 3:5). Jesus is the true and perfect One whose voice we must heed. He not only is our great example of godly living, He is also able to endow our lives with the righteousness of God (2 Cor 5:21).

How, then, can anyone hope to find favor and communion with a holy God? Do not our own sins disqualify us from finding any good from Him? The apostle John gives us the glorious truth. "If we walk in the light, as He is in the light ...

The blood of Jesus His Son cleanses us from all sin" (1 Jn 1:7)
We have been brought by grace into the light of His truth and
righteousness and we are privileged to walk every day in the
light of His presence. The cleansing power of Christ is at work
in us. "If we confess our sins, He is faithful and just to forgive
us our sins and to cleanse us from all unrighteousness" (1 Jn 1:9).
But if we refuse to acknowledge our sin, we are deceived and
deny the truth. We can't hide our sins from Him anyway, but
the miracle of mercy is that if we acknowledge with grief our
wrongdoing, relying on His grace to turn our hearts to seek only
what is pleasing to Him, we find both forgiveness and cleansing.
We have been given great assurance of this, because when we sin
we have a righteous one who is our advocate before the Father
(1 Jn 2:1–2). Jesus's death has covered over the guilt of our sin,
turning aside the wrath of God. And Christ's resurrection and
ascension into glory lift us up with Him into spiritual life in the
presence of God in the heavenly places.

You Know No God but Me!

Hosea 13:1–8

HOSEA CONCLUDES HIS lengthy exposition of Israel's spiritual treason here. He presents the crucial question repeated many times in Old Testament history, which is also the vitally important question in the life of every person in every age: which god shall we serve? The issue was Israel's idolatrous worship, deliberately rejecting the reign of the God of Abraham who had redeemed them from bondage in Egypt and claimed them as His own precious possession. Israel is the prodigal son who departs from the house of his Father's love and turns to the futility of serving other gods.

Again, Hosea appeals to Israel's glorious past. Ephraim, though only half of the tribe of Joseph, was the largest and most powerful of all the tribes of the nation Israel. They spoke with great authority and commanded respect among their brothers (Hos 13:1). But the nation turned to Baal worship, especially under the leadership of King Ahab (1 Kings 16:30–33). Hosea says they incurred guilt through Baal and died. Their worship of the wrong gods had killed them! Their death was a gradual process of weakening and decay over a period of two hundred years but eventually did lead to foreign invasion and destruction of the kingdom. Hosea's prophecy vividly documents the decline of the glorious nation, first by spiritual rebellion, then scandalous moral decline, corrupt leadership, economic and political failure, and finally military disaster.

The devastating effects of spiritual death are described in Hosea 13:2–3. There is no end to their sinning. They continually invent new idols to fulfill the desires of their rebellious hearts. Refusing to worship the God who created them, they create for themselves false gods that they can touch and see. They employ their God-given skill and appreciation of beauty in order to give glory only to themselves. Hosea 13:2 probably does not refer to human sacrifice but to men who offer sacrifice to manmade images of calves. Their show of devotion is like kissing animals that act only by instinct and have no understanding. They degrade themselves by worshiping created things! The summary of their life before God is given in Hosea 13:3: nothing substantial, nothing permanent, nothing of value. If we follow Ephraim by setting our hearts on the pursuits and priorities of this world in neglect of God, we are dead even while we live. Which god will we serve?

But God will not surrender His people to false gods without a fight! He lays claim to the heart loyalty of His covenant people in Hosea 13:4: "You know no God but me." There is no other God! All others are not gods at all! He is their God from out of Egypt. He is the God who chose Israel for His own possession, who redeemed the people out of bondage, who revealed His glory to them, and who promised to send rich blessings upon them. There is no other savior, no one else who can be their helper. He indeed had loved them through the hardship of the wilderness, fed them, cared for them, and sheltered them with His protection (Hos 13:5). Does not our God melt our hard hearts by revealing the riches of His infinite mercy and patience with His wayward children? Shall we not abandon all pretense of seeking ultimate fulfilment and satisfaction from our own wisdom and achievement? The riches of this world and the works of our hands cannot be our gods. We use all God's good and perfect gifts in joyful submission and thankful worship of our gracious God, who richly provides us with everything to enjoy. Which god will we serve?

For there is a danger in being full of God's blessings. Hosea says, "They were filled, and their heart was lifted up; therefore they forgot Me" (Hos 13:6). How strange that fixing our attention on God's blessings can cause us to forget the God who gives them. How dreadful if our hearts worship and serve the good gifts that God has created but refuse to acknowledge the Creator who gives them.

That God is greatly displeased with the sin of worshiping created things rather than the Creator, is evident in Hosea 13:7–8. The God who displayed His glory and power in Egypt is the judge of all the earth. He desires the undivided heart devotion of those called into His covenant grace. But the sin of worshiping the wrong god will inevitably lead to the encounter with His fierce wrath. He likens Himself to four wild beasts that are awesome in their power to kill and destroy. The only true and living God is zealous for the worship He so rightly and richly deserves. He will not share His glory with another. Which god will we serve?

All humankind is confronted with this fundamental necessity of coming into vital union and communion with the one true God. Paul states this clearly in 1 Timothy 2:3–6: "… it is pleasing in the sight of God our Savior, who desires all people to be saved and to come to the knowledge of the truth. For there is one

God, and there is one mediator between God and men, the man Jesus Christ, who gave himself as a ransom for all, which is the testimony given at the proper time."

From these words we must observe several things. First, there is only one God. He is the God revealed in the Bible. Whatever else people may choose to worship are false gods, and worshiping them leads to destruction. Second, there is only one way to come to this God. There is only one mediator who can bring us to God, the man Jesus Christ. Third, Jesus is the only Savior. He alone gave Himself as a ransom to bring us to God. His own life was the purchase price that paid the debt to justice for all our sins and reconciled us to God. Fourth, God is gracious. He desires all people to be saved and come to the knowledge of the truth. He freely offers the gift of forgiveness and salvation to all humankind. Fifth, God is faithful and true. He has testified that these things are sure and trustworthy. What He has promised He will fulfill.

Hosea pleads with his own nation to remember the gift of God's calling. "You know no God but me, and besides me there is no savior" (Hos 13:4). So "choose this day whom you will serve" (Joshua 24:15). Now this same urgent call comes to all of humanity. Only the grace and mercy of Jesus Christ meets our desperate need for reconciliation and peace with God our Creator. To turn away from Him to any other principle or prophet leads only to spiritual darkness. Jesus is the true God and eternal life. Therefore we must keep ourselves from idols (1 Jn 5:20–21).

I Shall Redeem Them from Death

Hosea 13:9–16

HOSEA 13:1 STATES that Ephraim (the kingdom of Israel) incurred guilt through Baal worship and died. Israel's covenant unfaithfulness through worship of false gods led to their spiritual death. Chapter 13 points to the process of national death and destruction resulting from spiritual decay. Hosea presents Israel as a culture of death that chooses death. But then suddenly there appears in Hosea 13:14 a shocking contradiction: "I shall ransom them from the power of Sheol; I shall redeem them from Death." This rich and glorious promise occurs so abruptly that it is clearly intended to startle us with the realization that God is going to do something completely wondrous and unexpected. God is going to triumph over our spiritual death! He will open a way, not only for the people of Israel, but for all of humanity to gain life in everlasting communion with Him. God's grace will have the final and decisive word in the life and destiny of His covenant people.

Hosea insists that his nation Israel is a culture of death that chooses death. Because they forgot their true God (Hos 13:6),

His coming will be as dangerous as ferocious beasts (Hos 13:7–8) ready to destroy them (Hos 13:9). The nation is against their helper (Hos 13:9), turning aside from the one who can bring deliverance. Beside God they have no savior (Hos 13:4), but they look for impotent kings to save their cities (Hos 13:10). Israel's history was full of unrighteous kings who seized power and who then were overthrown by even more wicked kings—who in turn were overthrown by still others. God set up their kings in His anger and deposed them in His wrath (Hos 13:10–11). Their sin is an established lifestyle and a delight to them, kept in store as a treasure (Hos 13:12). The prodigal son is unwise (Hos 13:13), refusing even the gift of life, foolishly choosing death. This is a tragic picture of people who have been called by God's name but now in rebellion against God are consciously choosing their own destruction.

But God interrupts the procession of death! He drops the bombshell of Hosea 13:14, not on those who are busily pursuing a course of death but on death itself. God shall buy them back from death! He shall break the power of the grave! God is the author and giver of life, who sent His Son into the world that we might have life abundantly. When we were dead in our trespasses and sins, He made us alive together with Christ. Because of His great love and mercy, He raised us up to heavenly life everlasting (Eph 2:1–6). He is the gracious Father (Lk 15:24) who rejoices that the prodigal son who was dead is alive again!

But can these dead bones really live? God alone knows how this is possible (Ezek 37:3). "Truly no man can ransom another, or give to God the price of his life, for the ransom of their life is costly and can never suffice, that he should live on forever and never see the pit" (Ps 49:7–9). God alone "gives life to the dead and calls into existence the things that do not exist" (Rom 4:17). Jesus said that he came "to give His life as a ransom for many" (Mk

10:45). It is God who speaks in Hosea 13:14: "I shall ransom …
I shall redeem …." Here is an earthshaking, life-giving, destiny-
altering promise! God can even taunt death! He renders powerless
the pain and desolation of death for those whom He redeems.

The last sentence in Hosea 13:14 is troubling: "Compassion is
hidden from my eyes." The word translated as "compassion" can
also mean "repentance." God is saying he will not change from His
declared purpose to destroy the power of death. Any possibility
of altering His promise is completely off His radar screen! God's
sovereign grace and infinite power will certainly prevail in the
deliverance of ruined sinners from death to everlasting life in
fellowship with the Father.

Hosea proclaims God's glorious promise, but it is so wonderful
that he seems to be struggling to believe it. As he looks at the nation
around him, he sees no hope of compassion, only the certainty
of coming judgment (Hos 13:15–16). He solemnly warns of the
necessity of repentance (Hos 14:1–3) and returning to the one true
God. He sees Ephraim's God-given fruitfulness and prestige being
squandered, its fountain of life drying up, and every precious thing
being lost (Hos 13:15). He sees continual guilt and rebellion against
God and he sees a terrible invasion, destruction, and death coming
upon the nation (Hos 13:16). He recognizes that God's judgment
is righteous, so how can there be compassion and redemption?

Yet God graciously preserved a remnant of the people of Israel
and miraculously called them to return from the exile. He turned
their hearts to repent of idolatry and to worship and serve only
the God of Israel. He wondrously preserved Israel so that spiritual
life would come to the whole world through the promise of the
coming Messiah. This wondrous promise of life from the dead is
fulfilled only in the life and finished work of Jesus Christ. Jesus
gave His life to ransom "people for God from every tribe and
language and people and nation" (Rev 5:9). The infinite ransom

price of His precious blood (1 Pet 1:18–19) purchased our freedom from slavery to sin and death. Jesus is the only one who could pay the costly ransom price so that we could live eternally and not be condemned.

Paul, in 1 Corinthians 15:52–55, teaches that at Christ's second coming the dead in Christ shall be raised imperishable (1 Cor 15:52). He teaches us that the victory over death is in fulfillment of Isaiah 25:8, "Death is swallowed up in victory," and Hosea 13:14, "O death, where is your victory? O death, where is your sting?" He follows with the words, "But thanks be to God who gives us the victory through our Lord Jesus Christ" (1 Cor 15:57). Paul proclaims the same great victory that Hosea prophesied! This astonishing promise is for both Jews and Gentiles, for all who trust in Christ for salvation. Christ alone has the power to destroy the power of death! And He accomplished it by submitting to death Himself and then rising from the dead. Peter declares, "God raised him (Christ) up, loosing the pangs of death, because it was not possible for him to be held by it" (Acts 2:24).

And Paul teaches: "For as by a man came death, by a man has come also the resurrection of the dead. For as in Adam all die, so also in Christ shall all be made alive. But each in his own order: Christ the first fruits, then at his coming those who belong to Christ" (1 Cor 15:21–23). Christ, through His death, has destroyed the one who has the power of death and freed "those who all their lives were held in slavery by their fear of death" (Heb 2:14–15 NIV).

Hosea proclaims Christ, the only redeemer of God's people! Christ alone can transform our life and our world from a culture of death to a kingdom of life. Hosea knew and trusted the hope of future redemption through Christ's death and resurrection. He did not hesitate to proclaim this sure and certain promise by the word of God, who cannot lie.

The Wonder of Repentance
Hosea 14:1–3

OFTEN WE DON'T understand the main intent of a book until we get to the final chapter. This certainly is true of Hosea's book. Chapters 4 through 13 are filled with a detailed account of Israel's sins and rebellion against the love of their God. The prophet employs every possible literary means to describe both their hideous offense and its dreadful result. We might conclude that the purpose of the book is only to announce severe condemnation. But this final chapter reveals that while the warnings of judgment are real, the goal of the book is clearly to call Israel to repentance and reconciliation with their God.

Hosea twice commands and urges the people of Israel to "return to the Lord" (Hos 14:1, 2). This is not a new idea, for this same exhortation is given in Hosea 3:5; 6:1, 10:12, and 12:6. But now Hosea concludes his book by proclaiming God's rich promise of mercy and blessing to those who turn away from their sinful rebellion and worship and serve the living God.

What a wonder is this gracious call to repentance! Repentance means confessing that we have stumbled because of our iniquity (Hos 14:1). Not only have we stumbled, but we have fallen. Now we lie guilty and helpless. Our love for our sin has triumphed over our love for God. Our great spiritual need is to forsake our sin and return to embrace the love of God. Our only hope is to cry out to God, "Take away all iniquity and receive us graciously" (Hos 14:2 NIV), because a merciful God is the only one who can answer that prayer. God indeed is gracious and will graciously receive sinners who return to him. Here is strong encouragement for all who seek to walk with God and serve Him, yet constantly struggle with sin! Our heavenly Father works wondrous repentance in sinners and rejoices over each one who truly repents.

The first wonder of repentance is the gift of a changed heart, a miracle that only God can perform. Hosea directs that they should "take with you words" (Hos 14:2). He gives a prayer of repentance (Hos 14:2–3), sincerely expressing a change of direction in our soul, returning to the God against whom we have rebelled. This prayer contains the request that God would "accept what is good" (Hos 14:2). The only good we have to offer to God is the good that He Himself has graciously imparted. In David's prayer of repentance (Ps 51:10–12), he asks, "Create in me a clean heart, O God, and renew a right spirit within me. Cast me not away from your presence, and take not your Holy Spirit from me. Restore to me the joy of your salvation, and uphold me with a willing spirit." He recognizes that only the working of God's Spirit in us can give a clean heart and a joyful, willing spirit. It is God alone who can lead us to repentance, and only His power endows us with a new heart filled with love and devotion, a renewed mind and a submissive will. These good gifts radically consecrate our inner life to God. Then we offer them back to Him in acceptable worship. God delights to accept the good gifts He has entrusted to us.

God's mercy to all who call upon Him for salvation is a wonder beyond our comprehension! The God who is judge of all the earth is also a merciful God. Hosea puts a prayer of great hope in the mouth of repentant people Hosea 14:3: "In you (God) the orphan finds mercy." We are all spiritual orphans because of our sin: lost, abandoned, uncared for, and without hope. Yet He remains faithful to be "the LORD our God" (Hos 14:1). He abides in His covenant claim upon us as people belonging to Him and gives us assurance that He has accepted us in His beloved Son. For Hosea is pointing to the fullness of God's wondrous mercy, revealed to us only in Jesus Christ.

How desperately we need the mercy of Christ! What hope Christ brings for those who are overwhelmed by the weight of their sin and fearful that God could never forgive them. The whole of humanity, lost in sinful rebellion, deserving only God's condemnation, can find hope of God's pardon and salvation in Christ our redeemer. We all, like Israel, are prodigal children, rejecting the Father's love, wandering away from our true home, lost in the confusion of this world's lies. God's mercy enables us to come to our senses, to arise and return to our Father, acknowledging our foolish rebellion and pleading with Him to take away our iniquity. What wondrous mercy!

Repentance is the pledge from a heart changed by the power of God. If we are committed to follow Christ, we must reject all that is not pleasing to Him. Repentance is not only a plea for pardon and a return to God but the pledge, in dependence on the grace of God, of new obedience to our new master.

The prayer Hosea gives contains three promises to the Lord (Hos 14:2–3) that issue from repentant hearts. These promises should not be thought of as negotiating for God's favor or seeking His goodwill with bribes. Rather, they express a heart commitment to serve the Lord only and a confidence that He will be sufficient for all our needs. Positively, there is a promise to offer to God the praise and prayer of our lips (Hos 14:2). Instead of offering bulls as burnt sacrifices, we bring the fruit of renewed hearts dedicated to Him. Hebrews 13:15 borrows this thought: "Through him (Jesus) then let us continually offer up a sacrifice of praise to God, that is, the fruit of lips that acknowledge his name." Only because of Jesus are we enabled to offer proper worship, the consecration of our heart, words, and life, to God alone.

Hosea also gives two negative promises of repentance (Hos 14:3). First, we pledge not to depend on the power and promise of this world. Israel had pursued alliance with Assyria, the world's superpower. But that had only led them into bondage under an ungodly foreign dictator. They had relied on military power (riding on horses) but had failed to trust in the Lord for deliverance. Secondly, we pledge not to worship our own work and achievement. The "work of our hands" (Hos 14:3) refers to their manmade idols but also to our pride when we exalt our own strength and ability while ignoring God who gives them. Returning to God means rejecting worldly wisdom and power and seeking the peace and security that only God can bring.

We should ponder the wonder that Hosea preached repentance for forty years, yet was largely ignored by the people of his day. Human hearts stubbornly resist what God sets forth as the gateway to restoration and blessing. How then can this wonder of repentance come about? In Acts 11:18 the believers glorified God, saying, "Then to the Gentiles also God has granted repentance that leads to life." It was a new and wondrous idea that the blessings of the Messiah would come to the whole world. But they did recognize that repentance is the gift of God, and by the power of the gospel Christ calls sinners to repentance and salvation.

I Will Love Them Freely

Hosea 14:4

HOSEA'S CONCLUDING WORDS to us are a message of glorious grace and hope for sinners! What treasure in all the world could ever be more precious than the assurance of God's love for us? The wonder of repentance reveals the far greater wonder of covenant blessing for all God's people. God's promise is that He will indeed receive with healing power all who come before Him with a humble and contrite heart. He will turn aside His anger, He will heal their rebellion and He will love them freely (Hos 14:4). What glorious hope this brings to every human soul who earnestly seeks reconciliation with God our Creator.

These concluding verses begin with three "I will" statements, which are astonishing promises of deliverance from the power of sin. These are followed by numerous "they shall" promises of resulting blessings from God's gracious hand. These promises must certainly have been a great comfort and encouragement to Israel in exile, predicting God's deliverance and continued grace to His covenant people. But the fullness of these promises points forward to the far greater redemption purchased for us by our Lord Jesus Christ. God preserved and restored Israel in order to fulfill His ultimate promise to send the Savior of the whole world. The wonder of Israel's restoration from captivity is a foreshadowing of our ultimate deliverance from bondage to sin and the reign of Satan. And these blessings come by the promise of God to all who call upon Christ for salvation.

"I will love them freely" (Hos 14:4). God's simple and wonderful promise is the enduring foundation for all the blessings of salvation. Undoubtedly this promise of the free love of God has been finally fulfilled in the coming of Jesus Christ into the world. 1 John 4:9–10 declares: "In this the love of God was made manifest among us, that God sent his only Son into the world, so that we might live through him. In this is love, not that we have loved God but that he loved us and sent his Son to be the propitiation for our sins." The coming of Christ to be the Savior of the world is convincing proof that "God is love" (1 Jn 4:8).

God's love is proclaimed as a sovereign decree. The King of the universe expresses His love as an act of His free will. There is nothing in us or in the whole universe that compels Him to act in love. God freely chooses to act only because of infinite, compassionate love at the heart of His being. God's free love in Christ is unlimited and unrestrained as it moves forth with life-transforming grace and power. He sends forth His love with power to heal our brokenness, demolish our enmity, rebuke our foolish rebellion, and restore us to Christ-centered wholeness.

God loves us freely, in that He loved us first. He did not wait for us to love Him and then return our love. God took the initiative in sending His Son into the world. God loves us freely, in that He gave us the very best. He gave His Son, the most precious gift possible. But far greater than that, He loves us freely even though we are completely unlovely and undeserving of His kindness because of our sin.

God's free love in Christ has fully healed our deepest need. By His grace His anger is turned away (Hos 14:4) and His power heals our apostasy. Hosea's pressing question is, who could ever turn aside God's righteous anger impending because of the wickedness of the people? In response, he must be pointing us to a Savior and deliverer whom God Himself would provide. Only by our Lord Jesus Christ can we be assured that God's anger has been turned away from us. He sent His Son as a propitiation for our sins, covering over our guilt, turning aside the wrath of God, and bringing reconciliation between God and us. And in His free love He brought about our highest good and blessing, that we might have heavenly life in Christ.

God says, "I will heal their apostasy" (Hos 14:4). Our hearts constantly wander away from devotion to our Savior God, seeking from the temporal idols of this world the deliverance and peace that can only be found in Christ. Only the love of the Son of God at work in our lives can heal both the symptoms and the root causes of apostasy. "The love of Christ controls us" (2 Cor 5:14), making us faithful and steadfast. Only Christ the great physician of souls can heal the heart; only in Him can our souls find rest and refuge from the continual dangers of false worship and futile philosophies.

Hosea's marriage and message declare the redeeming love of God for sinful people. That love has been ultimately revealed in the life and ministry of our Lord Jesus Christ. Only Christ is the perfect righteous one who completely fulfilled the righteousness of God's law for us. Only Christ has taken upon Himself the guilt of the sins of His people and has suffered the wrath of God that we deserved. His mercy has triumphed over justice for our eternal good.

Hosea's promise of God's free love is a reality that is infinitely beyond our ability to comprehend (Eph 3:18–19) but fills our existence with the presence and power of God. Hosea is the prophet of God's amazing love.

Every Spiritual Blessing
Hosea 14:5–9

THE CONCLUSION OF Hosea's book brings great comfort and hope by proclaiming God's wondrous blessings which He promises for His repentant people. This is such a sharp contrast to the dreadful threats of judgment in the rest of the book that we must wonder how such blessings are ever possible. Ultimately these are the blessings of the new covenant and are the outworking of God's love in Christ. God announces His intention to bring to His people in every nation and every age "every spiritual blessing in the heavenly places" in Christ (Eph 1:3).

God's first promise, "I will be like the dew to Israel" (Hos 14:5), sounds strange to our ears, but to the people of Hosea's day it made perfect sense. In the arid climate of Israel, rain was scarce in the growing season and dew was an essential source of the water of life for their crops. But Israel's problems were spiritual problems and demanded a spiritual solution. God's solution is to graciously give the abundant water of new spiritual life that could only come from the Messiah. Jesus (Jn 7:37–39) promises that rivers of living water will flow from the hearts of those who believe in Him. This describes the work of the life-giving Spirit of God, like a mighty flood of spiritual blessings, to all who trust in Christ for salvation. God's promise to be like the dew becomes assurance that the gift of the Holy Spirit will bring true life and rich spiritual fruitfulness to His people in Christ.

What follows in Hosea 14:5–8 is a picture of a rich, abundant, and luxuriant spiritual life produced in us by God's dew of life. Christ echoes this abundance of the life-giving Spirit in Matthew 13:23, where the seed sown on good soil "is the one who hears the word and understands it. He indeed bears fruit and yields, in one case a hundredfold, in another sixty, and in another thirty."

Hosea says repentant, forgiven people will be like the beauty and fragrance of the lily (Hos 14:5-6). Paul says believers in Christ are "the aroma of Christ to God," and that through us Christ "spreads the fragrance of the knowledge of him [God] everywhere" (2 Cor 2:14–15). He exclaims, "How beautiful are the feet of those who preach the good news" (Rom 10:15). Christians are to shine forth like stars in the universe (Phil 2:15). We are enabled to "worship the Lord in the beauty of holiness" (Ps 96:9 KJV).

Hosea says they "shall take root like the trees of Lebanon" (Hos 14:5), showing stability and firm standing. Paul says, "as you received Christ Jesus the Lord, so walk in Him, rooted and built up in Him and established in the faith" (Col 2:6–7). Christians are those who "are standing firm in one spirit, with one mind striving side by side for the faith of the gospel" (Phil 1:27).

Hosea says their "shoots shall spread out" (Hos 14:6). Jesus says the kingdom of God will grow like a tree with large branches (Mt 13:32). He tells His disciples that they shall be His witnesses to the end of the earth (Acts 1:8).

Hosea says they will dwell beneath God's shadow (Hos 14:7), a picture of protection, security, and peace. "Humble yourselves, therefore, under the mighty hand of God so that at the proper time he may exalt you, casting all your anxieties on him, because he cares for you" (1 Pet 5:6–7). Paul says, "The Lord will rescue me from every evil deed and bring me safely into his heavenly kingdom" (2 Tim 4:18). Jesus said, "I have said these things to you, that in me you may have peace. In the world you will have tribulation. But take heart; I have overcome the world" (Jn 16:33).

Hosea says "they shall flourish like the grain" (Hos 14:7). They shall be abundantly productive and fruitful. James 3:17–18 speaks of a far greater spiritual harvest: "But the wisdom from above is first pure, then peaceable, gentle, open to reason, full of mercy and good fruits, impartial and sincere. And a harvest of righteousness is sown in peace by those who make peace." Our lives are vitally transformed by the rich production of the fruit of the Spirit in us (Gal 5:22–23).

Hosea says, "their fame shall be like the wine of Lebanon" (Hos 14:7). The whole earth shall know and honor their integrity. Paul speaks of famous faith granted to the Thessalonians: "For not only has the word of the Lord sounded forth from you in Macedonia and Achaia, but your faith in God has gone forth everywhere, so that we need not say anything. For they themselves report concerning us the kind of reception we had among you, how you turned to God from idols to serve the living and true God …" (1 Thes 1:8–9). The wine Jesus produced (Jn 2:9–10) far exceeds in delight the wine of this present world, pointing to the unbounded rejoicing of the coming kingdom of righteousness and truth.

God speaks to Israel in Hosea 14:8: "I am like an evergreen cypress; from me comes your fruit." Jesus says, "I am the vine; you are the branches. Whoever abides in me and I in him, he it is that bears much fruit, for apart from me you can do nothing" (Jn 15:5). God's eternal riches for His people are pictured in the new holy city of Jerusalem (Rev 22:2), where the tree of life yields its fruit each month and its leaves are for the healing of the nations. Surely Hosea's promised showers of blessings are a prophecy of the glorious spiritual riches to come to all His people only through redemption in Jesus Christ.

The last two verses are a summary of the whole book of Hosea and a fitting appeal in light of his whole message. The question, "What have I to do with idols?" (Hos 14:8) may be understood as a declaration. "I will not compete with idols for the affection and heart-loyalty of my people." The choice is crystal clear. Either they must reject the idols of the nations, or God would reject them as His people. Hosea has consistently announced that idolatry was at the very core of Israel's spiritual weakness and would lead to her downfall. Now he sets forth the immense contrast between the true God and the idols of the nations. God has answered his people when they called upon Him; He is the God who has watched over them with care. From Him alone have come fruitful blessings. Worship of Baal has brought them no aid, no security, no peace. God calls us to steadfast devotion by promising: "I will love them freely" (Hos 14:4)

Hosea concludes his book by affirming the sweetness and blessing of all that God has said through His prophet. These truths are great riches to those who are wise and discerning. He says, "Whoever is wise, let him understand these things; whoever is discerning, let him know them; for the ways of the LORD are right, and the upright walk in them, but transgressors stumble in them" (Hos 14:9). The double use of the word "whoever" implies an open invitation to know and understand the full blessing of spiritual life and prosperity. He declares that all God's dealings with mankind, and all His directives for our lives, are righteous and good and profitable. Those whose hearts are transformed by God's grace to seek pardon for sins and communion with God will live in His grace and blessing. The alternative is to live in rebellion against God's word; the result will be to stumble and fall.

This choice proclaimed by Hosea is also set before the whole world in the gospel of Jesus Christ. Paul, in 1 Corinthians 1:23–24, declares: "... we preach Christ crucified, a stumbling block to Jews and folly to Gentiles, but to those who are called, both Jews and Greeks, Christ the power of God and the wisdom of God." Some find the gospel of Christ to be offensive or foolish, but God declares it to be His wise and powerful call to salvation and eternal life. In rich mercy God calls us to embrace Christ as our Savior who died to forgive our sins and deliver us from the coming wrath. He calls us to bow before Christ, the living Lord, committed with our whole heart to observe all He has commanded us. Let us respond in faith to His gracious call with joy and heartfelt gratitude and devotion, for God has indeed loved us freely and infinitely.

About the Author

Chris Liff is an elder of a Presbyterian congregation in Vermont. For over 30 years he has taught the Bible in adult Sunday school and small group studies. He is a retired high school math teacher.

Printed in the United States
by Baker & Taylor Publisher Services